Frozen Fields of Fire:

Fredericksburg

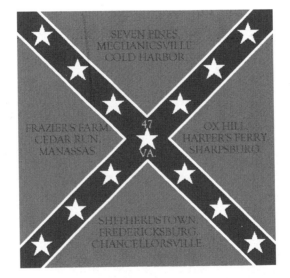

47th Virginia Infantry Regiment

Faye M. Benjamin

ISBN-13:
978-1511501835

ISBN-10:
1511501839

DEDICATION

This novel is dedicated to the re-enactors of the 47th Virginia Infantry Regiment. Through them, each generation gains insight into the American Civil War, and the horrific sacrifices that generation endured including both soldiers, sailors, marines and civilians.

In memory of the men who served honorably in the 47th Virginia Infantry Regiment.

BOOKS BY FAYE M. BENJAMIN

Freestone Series

Book 1 - <u>The Terrible Three and Murder</u>
Book 2 - <u>Judgment Leads to Murder</u>
Book 3 - <u>Shower Curtain Killer</u>
Book 4 – <u>Murdered by Mistake</u>
Book 5 – <u>Who Is Stalking Me?</u>

<u>Civil War Series</u>

Book 1 – <u>River of Tears</u>
Book 2 – <u>Lost Drummer Boy</u>
Book 3 – <u>Frozen Fields of Fire: Fredericksburg</u>

ACKNOWLEDGMENTS

Thanks to the Library of Congress and Wikipedia for the maps, photos, and art work used in this novel.

Thanks to the 47th Virginia Infantry Regiment Re-enactors for all their help and encouragement to make this novel possible.

LIST OF CHARACTERS

Judge Arthur Murphy/Vera Murphy
David Murphy/Kathleen Murphy/Andrew
Aaron Murphy/Deidre Murphy/ Belle
Grace & Teddy Murphy
Homer Murphy/Ellen Henley Murphy
Clay & Gus Henley
Ty & Harry Murphy
Micah Johnson
George & Luella Moss
Abner/ Eva/ Richard Moss
Joseph Bishop
Elisha/Minnie/Jonas Davis
Dr. Gabriel Hayden

CHAPTER 1

Fate comes like a thief in the night. As the angry clouds of war kept gathering across the nation, two brothers, their two cousins, and their friends in Virginia wonder which candidate will be elected President of the United States. If Abraham Lincoln is elected President, the friends know the Lower South will secede from the Union. They believe Virginia will secede, also. If war should come, what were the friends going to do?

The friends didn't know that fate was going to descend upon the small town of Fredericksburg, Virginia and the surrounding counties with devastating fury. The townspeople and their neighbors will be pushed to the brink of total disaster as they struggle to stay alive. What will they have to do in order to survive?

Arthur and Vera Murphy live in Fredericksburg, Virginia where Arthur is a judge. They have four children: 22 year old David, 20 year old Aaron, 16 year old Grace, and 9 year old Teddy. David is married to Kathleen Watson, and Aaron is married to Deidre Jones. Both men work for Amos Archer as bricklayers and carpenters. Both men live in modest homes on the outskirts of the town.

The Murphy family gathered for a picnic at Arthur's home one Sunday in September of 1860.

Teddy ordered, "Don't you eat all the chicken legs, David!"

David teased, "You've already eaten five legs, boy!"

"No, I haven't. I've only had two."

Aaron swatted Teddy's behind and teased, "You can't have anymore, because you look like a chicken leg."

"No, I don't! Mama says I'm handsome!"

Aaron teased, "She says that, because you're her baby boy!"

Vera jumped in, "All my boys are handsome, and my daughter is beautiful."

David called for everybody's attention and took his wife's hand.

"Kathleen and I have some good news to announce. She's having a baby in February."

Everyone gathered around the couple and hugged them senseless. This would be Arthur and Vera's first grandchild. Arthur broke out a bottle of wine, so everybody could toast the coming baby. Even Teddy got a very small glass to toast.

The family enjoyed a wonderful day together. The ladies were putting the food away while the men gathered in the living room to discuss the troubling events happening around them.

David asked, "Do you think Stephen Douglas will win the presidential election?"

Arthur answered, "I think the election will come down to Douglas or Lincoln."

Aaron added, "If Lincoln wins and Virginia secedes, David and I are going to enlist, if our state needs us!"

Arthur responded, "I want you two to make your own decisions. If war is declared, I expect you to do your duty and not shame your family. I want you to be men of honor."

David remarked, "We won't let you down, Poppa."

Grace looked at her mother in the kitchen and said, "I'm so happy for David and Kathleen. I know he'll be a good father."

Vera responded, "They'll both be wonderful parents. It'll be a blessing to have my grandchild running around the house."

Grace told her mother, "Go sit down in the living room and visit. I'll finish up in here."

"I'm going to get your father, so he can bring down Teddy's crib for them. I still have some blankets and baby clothes I can bring down."

"That's a wonderful idea, Mama!"

Arthur got the crib from the attic, and Vera got the clothes and blanket. The proud grandpa-to-be smiled as he brought down the crib.

All of a sudden, Vera tripped on the stairs and started falling down the steps. The women screamed as Arthur dropped the crib and tried to break her fall. David launched himself towards his mother and caught her before she hit the bottom step.

Arthur yelled, "Aaron, get the doctor!"

He ran out of the house and raced down the street.

Teddy started crying and asked, "Mama, what's wrong?"

Arthur took his wife in his arms and pleaded, "Come on honey talk to me."

He felt for a pulse in her neck, but he couldn't feel one. He put his ear to her chest, but he didn't hear anything. Tears started rolling down his cheeks when he realized she wasn't breathing.

Teddy wept and pleaded, "Mama get up! Please get up!"

Grace held her brother in her arms as they both cried.

Aaron and the doctor rushed into the house. Once the doctor examined Vera, he knew she was dead.

He said, "I'm so sorry, Arthur. Vera's neck is broken. I wish there was something I could do to bring her back."

Teddy pleaded, "Come back, Mama! I don't want you to leave!"

Grace looked at her brother and said, "Mama has gone to heaven. You and I have to be strong and help Poppa."

He asked, "Do you mean to take care of Poppa?"

"Yes, we have to be brave and make sure Poppa doesn't have to worry about us."

David held his pregnant wife and sobbed, "It was such a wonderful day."

Kathleen reminded him, "At least, she knew she was going to be a grandmother. That brought her great joy."

Aaron wiped tears and told his father, "We'll help you, Poppa."

Deidre commented, "Grace, we'll help you and Teddy. All of us will work together."

Arthur took Grace and Teddy into his arms and said, "Grace, you are the woman of the house, now. Teddy, you must help Grace take care of our home. Be a good son and do what she asks you to do."

Teddy answered, "I will, Poppa. I'm going to take care of you and Grace. I want Mama to be proud of me."

Several days later, Vera Murphy was buried in the church cemetery surrounded by her family and friends. Arthur's brother, Homer, and his family attended the funeral after arriving from Caroline County.

Homer owns a good sized farm that he and his family work. On the side, he raises and sells chickens and eggs. His wife, Ellen, has two sons from her first marriage named Clay and Gus. Homer and Ellen have a fourteen year old daughter named Leann, an eleven year old son named Ty, and a five year old son named Harry.

That evening, the families of Arthur and Homer gathered at Arthur's home for dinner and a visit.

Homer commented, "Arthur, I'm worried about the election coming up and all the useless debate going on in Congress. Two senators even got into a fight in the Capitol over a slavery speech. Mark my words, our nation is headed for war."

Arthur replied, "I feel the same way. If Lincoln is elected, the Lower South will secede in a hurry."

Clay added, "You can bet more states will secede including Virginia. Lincoln's troops will march into our state to protect Washington, D. C."

Gus went on, "Virginia will need her men to organize an army to beat back the federal troops. They'll be invading our land and homes."

Homer continued, "I'm sure, as soon as Virginia secedes and joins the Lower South, she'll start raising an army."

David remarked, "Our state could turn into a giant battlefield."

Clay laughed and said, "We'll whip the Union troops in no time. Their bodies will litter the ground."

Aaron asked, "Are ya'll going to join up?"

Gus answered, "You bet we are! None of us will fight against our state and homes!"

Arthur asked, "Will you be able to work your farm when the boys join up?"

Homer responded, "I believe so. Ty and Harry are old enough to work the farm, now."

Ty jumped in, "I'm already working with Clay to learn how to do things, and I'm 11 years old."

Harry chimed in, "Gus is teaching me how to be a farmer. Ty and I are real strong. I'm five years old and big for my age."

Leann commented, "Don't forget about me. I work with the chickens and help Mama in the house."

Clay teased, "She sure has a way with the chickens. Just call her the Chicken Queen."

Gus teased, "She's Queen Leann Chicken."

Everyone laughed while she stuck her tongue out.

Grace suggested, "Don't pay any attention to all those silly boys!"

Ellen told her daughter, "Honey, the men are just jealous you can sweet talk more eggs out of those chicken's behinds than they can."

Clay blabbed, "Uncle Arthur, can you believe she pets and talks to those chickens like they are people?"

"If that works, then I'd say keep talking to them."

Leann shot back, "Thank you, Uncle Arthur."

Gus teased, "She has chickens following her all over the place. She probably sleeps with some of them."

Teddy asked, "How many chickens do you have?"

"We have about 75 chickens."

Grace reacted, "Lord have mercy, that's a lot!"

The family gathered at the tables to enjoy a special meal together. Their friends and church members brought a lot of food to the family to help Grace now that her mother was gone.

Homer went on, "We are getting ready in case war is declared. We're cutting down a lot of trees in the middle of my wooded property to use as firewood and to build chicken coops. If we need to hide chickens from the Yankees, that's where they'll go."

Ellen added, "You know them Yankees will steal anything they can get their hands on, Arthur. Are you going to stock up?"

He answered, "Our homes will only hold so much, but we'll start collecting extras."

Homer offered, "If your family ever needs a place, you come on down, and we'll work together. Lord knows, what this war will have in store for us."

Ellen asked, "Teddy, would you like to spend some time on the farm with us?"

"I guess so, but I have to take care of Grace and Poppa."

"Well, anytime you want to come you'll be welcomed."

Grace replied, "Thanks Aunt Ellen, that means a lot to us."

The following day, Homer's family left to head back home. Two of David's friends stopped by Arthur's home to leave some food their mothers had cooked. Grace thanked them for being such caring neighbors and friends. Grace knew both of them would probably join up if war descended on the nation and their state.

Micah Johnson noticed how cute Grace was now that she was sweet sixteen. When she was a kid, she was skinny, awkward, and kind of homely looking. Her pig tails were gone, and her hair was a long, wavy, auburn brown. He would love to touch and run his fingers through it. He never noticed how long her eye lashes were before. Her blue eyes seemed to dance and sparkle.

He thought, "What is wrong with me? I'm going to be a soldier and go off to war. I don't have time for romance. Right now, the last thing I need is a wife!"

After the friends left, Grace wondered why Micah kept looking at her. She hoped she didn't have a bug in her hair. Lord sakes, she would be so embarrassed.

During November of 1860, fate descended on the nation. Most every household felt like a volcano was ready to explode. The nation's destiny was on the doorstep.

When Abraham Lincoln was elected President of the United States, tension invaded most every household in the South.

South Carolina wasted little time and seceded on December 20, 1860. Quickly, the Lower South followed with Mississippi seceding on January 9, 1861, Florida seceding on January 10th, and Alabama seceding on January 11th. Georgia and Louisiana seceded towards the end of January. Texas seceded on February 1st and joined the Confederacy.

On February 11, 1861, David and Kathleen had a baby boy they named Andrew. Thankfully, mother and son were doing well. Arthur was a proud grandfather and wished Vera could have held the baby in her arms.

As winter gave way to spring, tension gripped most every household. The Confederate states took over federal arsenals and several forts in the South. They demanded President Lincoln withdraw federal troops stationed in forts in Confederate territory.

By April, 1861, South Carolina demanded the federal

troops at Fort Sumter in Charleston Harbor be withdrawn. When that didn't happen, Confederate forces bombarded Fort Sumter on April 12th. There was no turning back, now. War descended on the two nations with a ruthless fury.

Arthur's older sons and their wives arrived at their father's home with news that would change their lives forever.

Aaron stated, "President Lincoln has called for 75,000 volunteers to put down the rebellion. David and I are going to enlist in the Stafford Guards in Stafford County."

Arthur told them, "Do your best and be men of honor. I just heard Virginia seceded on April 17th."

David remarked, "We're going to enlist the 22nd of April."

Arthur continued, "I want Kathleen, the baby, and Deidre to live with us. I want all my family together."

David responded, "Thank you, Poppa. We were hoping you would keep an eye on our wives."

Arthur suggested, "Close up your homes and bring all your valuables here. Teddy and I will take a bedroom, Deidre and Grace can share another bedroom, and Kathleen and the baby can set up in the third bedroom."

When Virginia joined the Confederacy, and Richmond became the capitol of the Confederate states, they wanted to stop goods and supplies from reaching Washington, D. C. Batteries were set up along the Potomac River to fire on any enemy shipping before they could reach the Chesapeake Bay. Batteries were set up at Freestone Point in Prince William County, Cockpit Point near Evansport (Quantico), Aquia Landing in Stafford County, and Mathias Point in King George County.

President Lincoln and the War Department knew they had to keep the Potomac River and Chesapeake Bay open. They couldn't let the Confederates blockade Washington, D. C. If that happened, supplies would have to come from Baltimore, Maryland.

The Department of the Navy created the Potomac Flotilla to keep the Potomac River channel and the Chesapeake Bay open. Their job was to destroy the Confederate batteries along the shorelines and sink enemy shipping.

When April 22nd came around, Homer's and Arthur's families gathered in Fredericksburg to say goodbye to four of their men that were joining the Stafford Guards. Arthur's sons closed up their homes and moved their wives and grandson into his home. David and Aaron wanted their wives with family while they went off to war. David knew his father would take care of Kathleen and Andrew. Aaron didn't want Deidre living alone during times like these.

Homer's stepsons, Clay and Gus, weren't married yet, so the men wouldn't have to worry about wives left behind.

Three friends that were close to the Murphy and Henley boys were joining up with them. Micah Johnson, Abner Moss, and Joseph Bishop joined the picnic at Arthur's place.

Abner commented, "I hope the war isn't over by the time we get trained."

Gus bragged, "When we get in the fight, it won't be

long before we picnic at the White House."

Joe added, "I sure would like to hog tie President Lincoln all by myself."

Arthur suggested, "The Union already has an army. Those soldiers will fight, so don't expect them to surrender after the first shot is fired."

Gus blabbed, "Most of them are city boys. They don't know how to shoot a deer let alone a person."

David teased, "Gus, you sure are mighty high on yourself."

He replied, "I can shoot better than you!"

Aaron continued, "Once all of us are trained, we should be right good at shooting."

Clay chimed in, "Gus always has a big mouth. He'll probably mess in his pants the first time a Yankee fires at him!"

Gus shot back, "Go jump on a picket fence, Clay!"

Ellen commented, "You boys better not get too cocky, because I want both of you to come home."

Clay answered "Don't worry Mother, we will."

Teddy ordered, "Bring me back a Yankee sword."

David swatted his behind and said, "Those swords are bigger than you are."

He fired back, "I'm getting bigger all the time."

Homer suggested, "Our boys will be busy fighting. They won't have time to look for souvenirs. Besides, that could get them killed."

Teddy answered, "Sorry, I didn't think about that."

Arthur called the group together and said, "I'm giving each one of you a knife to carry with you. One can always use a knife for almost any job. I pray these will help protect you."

Aaron responded, "Father, these knives are a

wonderful gift. I've never seen any with such fancy engravings on them. I'll cherish mine always."

Micah replied, "Thank you so much, Judge Murphy. This knife is magnificent, and I'll cherish mine, too."

All the boys were shocked to receive a 12-inch knife in an ornate scabbard. Shoot fire! A person could chop down small trees with it and shave.

Micah wanted to talk to Grace alone somewhere, but he never got a chance to say anything. The time came for the boys to leave with Mr. Johnson. There were many hugs, kisses, and tears shed by all. Even Teddy cried when he hugged David and Aaron goodbye.

Micah was able to steal a hug from Grace.

He whispered in her ear, "I will miss you terribly, Grace. Please think of me often."

He kissed her forehead and jumped up into his father's wagon. When the wagon left, Kathleen sobbed in Arthur's arms while Deidre, Grace, and Teddy held on to each other and cried.

Homer stroked his wife's hair as she cried in his arms. Leann held on to her brothers as they wept and wiped tears.

This kind of scene was happening in thousands of households in the North and South. Their young men were so sadly unprepared for the chaos and carnage that awaited them. What did trench warfare mean to them? What did footsore and exhausted mean to them? Did they realize how many of them would die from disease? Not one of those young men had any idea the war would drag on for four long and bitter years.

CHAPTER 2

The carefree men were mustered into the
30th Virginia Infantry in Company I. They were sent to
Aquia Landing, not only as infantry, but to man artillery
batteries on shore to fire on and sink enemy shipping.
Secondly, they were to keep the Richmond,
Fredericksburg, and Potomac Railroad open for
Confederate use only. In other words, no supplies were
to get to Washington, D. C. by the railroad.

The men trained, went about their duties, and kept
their camp in good order. Their biggest shock was the
quality and quantity of the food. It sure didn't taste like
mama's home cooking. The men supplemented their
diet by hunting, fishing, and running trap lines. At least,
they wouldn't starve to death.

One evening the boys were eating a fine meal of fried
fish.
Between bites David commented, "I hear our spies
have gotten rid of all the buoys from the river. That
means the Yankee ships might run aground."
Gus chimed in, "Ain't that a real shame. If they run
aground close enough to us, we can blow them out of
the water."
Clay added, "It was nice to hear the fine folks of
Virginia approved the secession bill on May 23rd."
Aaron went on, "Virginia was not going to send
troops to President Lincoln to attack the Lower South."
Abner said in disgust, "You see what happened, don't
ya? President Lincoln sent troops to take over
Arlington and Alexandria."

Joe fired back, "I'd say Virginia has been invaded."

Micah asked, "Do you think the Yankees will try to attack our shore batteries and land troops from their boats?"

Clay answered, "They probably will. We have guns by the river and guns on Split Rock Bluff that commands the channel. There ain't no way they can get through us."

On May 29, 1861, the *USS Thomas Freeborn* attacked Aquia Landing. The Union vessel fired about fourteen shots on the batteries, but it didn't amount to much.

The following day, the *USS Thomas Freeborn,* the *USS Anacostia*, and the *USS Resolute* fired on the Confederate batteries at Aquia with little success.

On June 1st, the three Union vessels along with the *USS Pawnee* fired 500 shells on the Aquia batteries for five hours. They only managed to damage a few buildings, some railroad tracks, and kill one horse and chickens.

On June 27, 1861, the *USS Thomas Freeborn* returned to do battle at Mathias Point in King George County. They were going to land sailors and marines to set up a battery on the point and disable the Confederate cannons.

Four companies of the 30th Virginia fell into ranks commanded by Maj Robert Mayo.

He addressed his men, "We are ordered to Mathias Point to help their garrison beat back a Yankee landing party. We can't let the Yankees set up a battery on the point."

The boys realized this could be combat up close and personal. Firing at ships was one thing, but a landing party was entirely different.

David thinks, "Can I shoot a man that's looking into my eyes?"

Clay thinks, "I'm ready and itching for a fight!"

Micah thinks, "I must be brave and do my duty."

Abner believes, "It's time to fight, because I'm tired of training."

Joe is nervous, afraid, and wonders if he's going to die. He wonders what it feels like to get shot.

When the companies got there, they formed up for a counterattack. They fired volley after volley and forced the landing party to retreat to their boats while their ship tried to cover the retreat.

The men fired at the boat as well as the landing party.

Gus sees a sailor fall while manning a deck gun and yells, "We hit the gunner!"

The companies keep firing and another gunner falls to the deck. Commander James Ward was mortally wounded while manning a deck gun. The Union would suffer four wounded and one killed.

Clay yells, "They're pulling away and heading for the channel!"

David looked at his brother, Aaron, and asked, "Are you alright?"

"I guess so. My heart is racing, I'm burning up, and my hands are still shaking."

David added, "I feel the same way. I could drink a bucket full of water."

Gus looked at Joe and asked, "What are you laughing about?"

"We beat the pants off of them. This was a lot of fun.

It was like hunting and shooting a deer."

Micah grabbed Joe by his jacket and shouted, "I better not hear you say that again! Shooting to kill human beings isn't fun! I pray to God he'll forgive me for taking a life. You shouldn't take pleasure in killing!"

Joe fired back, "Mind your own business, Micah!"

Battle of Mathias Point

The garrison at Aquia Landing set about constructing two more batteries on Brent Point to cover the Aquia Creek and on a cliff near Aquia.

In July, the garrison put mines in the river near Aquia Landing made from 80-gallon barrels holding a boiler-iron torpedo filled with gunpowder. Unfortunately for the Confederates, Union sailors saw the devices floating in the river and were able to remove them before any ships were sunk.

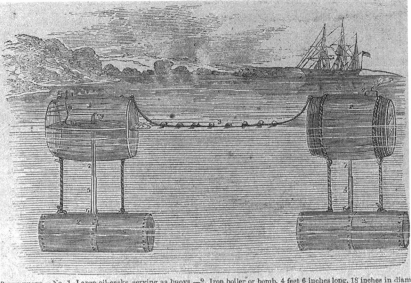

Photo # NH 59384   Confederate mine "picked up on the Potomac" by USS Pawnee, 1861

REFERENCES.—No. 1. Large oil-casks, serving as buoys.—2. Iron boiler or bomb, 4 feet 6 inches long, 18 inches in diam eter.—3. Rope 3 inches, with large pieces of cork at a distance of every 2 feet.—4. Box on top of cask, with fusee.—5. Gutta-percha tube fitting in to copper pipe—6. Brass tap on bomb.—7. Copper tube running through cask.—8. Wood on platform in centre of casks, in which fusee was coiled and secured.—9. Fusee.

INFERNAL MACHINE PICKED UP ON THE POTOMAC BY THE U. S. STEAMER "PAWNEE."

Floating mines

After September 1861, Company I became part of the 47th Virginia Infantry Regiment commanded by Col George Richardson. For the rest of the year and until March 1862, the 47th Virginia continued to man the garrison at Aquia Landing.

After the first Battle of Bull Run, both sides knew they had made a lot of mistakes. Most Union and Confederate troops from privates to officers were poorly trained. Many officers were elected by their companies or were political appointees with no military experience. Officers and enlisted men needed proper training.

On the Bull Run battlefield, uniforms were all different colors, so it was almost impossible to determine which units were friend or foe.

The South lost the chance to chase the Union forces back to Washington, D. C. and enter the city, because their army was in chaos and needed to regroup.

President Lincoln appointed Gen George McClellan to train the Union army, properly, and turn the Army of the Potomac into a well-trained and supplied unit. All the regiments sent by the different states had to work together as one.

The South faced many of the same problem, but with less men to enlist and the increasing lack of war supplies.

President Lincoln wanted Gen McClellan to destroy the Confederate batteries along the Potomac River and move against Richmond by March 1862.

President Abraham Lincoln   Gen George McClellan

The 47th Virginia Infantry of nearly 1,000 men left the coast and started marching towards Richmond. The regiment would never have that many men again.

When they got to Richmond, the regiment was loaded on boats and sent down the James River close to Yorktown.

While camped at Lee's Farm, the regiment voted Maj Robert Mayo the new commanding officer of the regiment.

The regiment spent May 2nd through May 4th camped behind Lebanon Church.

The men sat around the campfire thinking about the last few months.

David commented, "Our company has been lucky, so far. Only Pvt Fielding Knoxville, Pvt Amos Fritter, and Pvt Elijah Knoxville have died from disease."

Gus added, "We've only had three men desert."

Clay went on, "When a soldier ain't no count, he might as well desert."

Micah remarked, "I don't want no chicken standing next to me in battle. The fool could get me killed."

Abner chimed in, "Amen to that!"

A soldier close by pulled out his banjo and started playing. The men sang, clapped, and danced to the music. That precious time gave the men a break from the tension of war.

Gen Joseph Johnston pulled his 10,000 men out of Yorktown and marched towards Richmond. After midnight on May 5th, the 47th Virginia was ordered to form part of the rear guard of the army.

Gus complained, "We can barely see where we're going! I might step on a snake, and I hate snakes."

Clay asked, "Where are we marching, now?"

David answered, "Somebody said something about

West Point."

Joe fumed, "Don't tell me we have to march all the way to New York!"

Aaron fired back, "For Pete's sake! We're headed to West Point, Virginia!"

Micah complained, "We marched to Richmond, and they threw our behinds on boats to Yorktown. Now, we're going back towards Richmond. I wish the generals would make up their cotton picking minds!"

Abner complained, "Here we are, a part of the rear guard eating everybody else's dust. The Yanks know where we are, because all we do is cough and spit!"

David added, "Sometimes, the dust makes us look like walking ghosts."

Aaron laughed and shot back, "I just thought about a perfect battle plan. The next time we look like this, we'll attack the Yanks and scare the living bejesus out of them!"

Micah blabbed, "If your plan works, they'll make you a general."

Gus chimed in, "Before you become a general, I want to wash all this dust off me in the York River when we get to West Point."

Abner teased, ""Oh no you don't Gus. You can't wash in the river, because you'll kill all the fish!"

Joe went on, "We'll catch a mess of fish, then we'll plop in the river."

From May 5th through May 8th, the rear guard and the 47th Virginia marched westward towards Richmond and made camp near New Kent Court House. The men were getting slim rations, due to supply wagons and commissary foul ups.

Gen Johnston's army was just outside Richmond by

May 18th.

Gen McClellan's army slowly marched up the Peninsula, and by May 30th, he had built bridges across the Chickahominy River. Part of his army was on the northern side of the river, and the other two corps were on the southern side. McClellan was not prepared for the Virginia weather that dumped sheets of rain on the clay soil and turning the Chickahominy River into a raging river. Many of the bridges washed away, and the soil turned into swamps and dangerous bogs.

Gen Joseph Johnston   Gen Stonewall Jackson

On May 31st, Gen Gustavus Smith's division, along with the 47th Virginia, was ordered to march down the muddy Nine Mile Road to Fair Oaks. Gen Johnston wanted to attack the two Union corps south of the Chickahominy River. However, this day would turn into one missed opportunity and one blunder after another.

Gen Stonewall Jackson's boys were supposed to march down Nine Mile Road by way of Charles City Road. Instead, they ended up on Williamsburg Road.

The attack was supposed to start around 8:00 am, but

nothing happened until 1:00 pm. Confederate Gen D. H. Hill got tired of waiting and ordered his men to attack.

Gen Johnston Pettigrew's brigade was waiting on Nine Mile Road near New Bridge Road, including the 47th Virginia, for orders. Finally, they were ordered to attack around 4:00 pm. Gen Smith's division marched towards the Union lines south of the Chickahominy River.

Gen D. H. Hill

Gen Johnston Pettigrew

Lt William Stewart from Company I yells, "Steady men! Dress the line! Let's push the Yanks into the river. Make every shot count!"

David thinks, "Lord is it hot! Sweat's pouring in my eyes! Why do I have a knot in my throat?"

Joe thinks, "It's about time we pitched into the Yanks."

The crack of infantry fire explodes. The smell of gunpowder hangs in the humid air. Suddenly, a soldier falls back against Clay and knocks him down.

Clay thinks, "Oh God, part of his face is gone. His blood and skin are on me. Sweet Jesus, he's dead! I got to get away from him!"

Gus grabs his brother and helps him up. Their line fires a volley and reloads.

Aaron thinks, "Reload! Why are my hands shaking? Easy! Git control of yourself."

Micah yells, "We're taking fire from two sides!"

David sees Pvt John Bryant shot in the left hand, and Abner sees Pvt Noah Jones shot in the neck.

The brigade answers the fire from both sides. Orders are yelled that most can't hear.

Abner fires a shot and while reloading, his ramrod is shot right out of his hand. He sees a young soldier on the ground next to him clawing at the grass.

He asks, "Are you hit?"

When he got no answer, he rolled the boy over only to see him shot in the stomach.

The young private grabbed Abner with a bloody, shaking hand and pleaded, "Please tell my mother I love her and I was brave."

The young boy shook a little, coughed, and slipped away. Tears rolled down Abner's face. He would never forget the look on that boy's face. He was shocked back to reality when a couple of soldiers ran pass him in retreat.

The 47th Virginia came under murderous fire from two sides. Without reinforcements the men pulled back taking cover wherever they could find it. Before 6:00 pm, Gen Smith ordered his division back to Nine Mile Road.

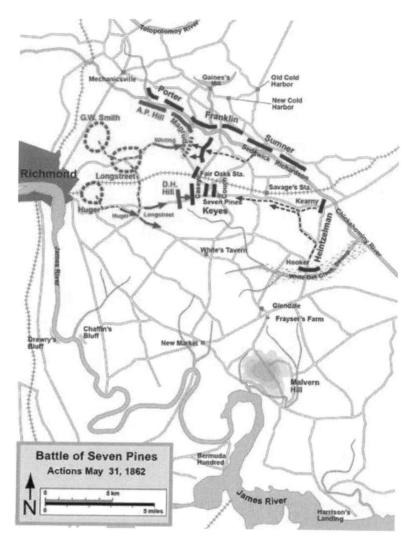

Battle of Seven Pines
Actions May 31, 1862

That evening, Gen Joseph Johnston was wounded and taken to Richmond. On June 1st, President Jefferson Davis appointed Gen Robert E. Lee commander of the Army of Northern Virginia. Now, it was up to Gen Lee to drive Gen McClellan off the Peninsula.

President Jefferson Davis   Gen Robert E. Lee

The men in the 47th Virginia who were killed during the Battle of Seven Pines were Pvt John Deshazo Co. A, Sgt George Kelly Co. A, Pvt Henry Lewis Co. B, Pvt Henry Payne Co. A, and Pvt George White Co. C (who was killed taking the wounded Gen Pettigrew from the battlefield).

While Gen McClellan fiddled his offensive plans away and became very cautious, Gen Lee spent valuable time building defensive fortifications almost 30 miles long from Richmond to Chaffin's Bluff on the James River. This break in the Peninsula Campaign gave Gen Lee time to plan his offensive to put the fear of the heavens into Gen McClellan making him think Lee's army was much larger than his.

Around the middle of June, the 47th Virginia was reassigned to Gen A. P. Hill's Light Division in the First Brigade commanded by Gen Charles Field. His brigade was made up of all Virginia regiments from the 22nd, 40th, 47th, 55th, and the 60th.

Gen A. P. Hill   Gen Charles Field

Aaron complained, "The men in our regiment are dropping like rain from all kinds of diseases. Most of them have typhoid."

Micah asked, "Who's sick in our company?"

He answered, "Chaplain Meredith said Sgt Jones, Cpl Stewart, Pvt Barber, Pvt James Dent, Pvt John Jones, Pvt Mountjoy, Pvt Smith, Pvt Stewart, and Pvt Jonas Jones are in the hospital."

Abner asked, "Has anybody died?"

He answered, "The chaplain said, "Pvt Wilson, Pvt Elijah Groves, Pvt Masters, and Pvt James Musselman have died."

Gus asked, "How are the wounded?"

He responded, "They are recovering."

David commented, "I hope we don't get sick."

Gen Lee knew if he captured Gen McClellan's supply base on the York River, then Gen McClellan couldn't attack Richmond. So, on June 24th, orders were issued to get the offensive plan moving.

Gus complained, "I'm tired of digging ditches, because

my hands have blisters on top of blisters."

Aaron teased, "Gus, all of us have blisters. I don't have soft hands anymore. Mine feel like tree bark."

David remarked, "At least, we're on the march and out of those ditches."

Micah added, "There must be 100,000 mosquitoes around here. I hate them, and the lice, ticks, and chiggers. I feel like one big bug bite."

Abner responded, "Amen to that! I wish they would only bite the Yanks."

Clay mentioned, "I hate the snakes! I almost stepped on one the other day, so I beat the living crap out of it. It sure didn't look like a snake after I finished beating it to death."

David suggested, "Keep a sharp lookout for them around the rivers and swamps."

Joe complained, "Don't tell me we're stomping around the swamps! It's hot as hades."

Aaron went on, "The lieutenant said we're marching to a place called Meadow Bridge."

Gus complained, "If bridge is in the name, you can bet water's involved."

Joe threatened, "If I see a snake, I'm going to shoot it plum dead."

Clay complained, "It seems like all we do is cough, spit, scratch bug bites, and pick varmints off our bodies."

Aaron reminded, "If we stomp through water, we better not forget about the leeches."

Gus commented, "I enjoy burning them off and smashing them with my musket butt."

Clay said in disgust, "I'll never forget having to burn them off. My hairy chest almost went up in flames."

Aaron asked, "Abner, why are you limping some?"

"I got blisters from these no count shoes."

Micah suggested, "Maybe, you can find a better pair if we go into battle."

The lieutenant shouted, "Halt! Grab something to eat. Dismissed!"

On the 26th of June, Gen A. P. Hill's division was on the southern end of Meadow Bridge waiting for the order to attack.

Abner asked, "Why are we waiting around doing nothing, sir?"

The lieutenant answered, "We're waiting for orders to attack from Gen Jackson."

Gen Hill told his aide, "I don't know why Gen Jackson isn't here, so we're going to attack, anyway."

Scouts came back to let Gen Hill know there were Union pickets near the bridge and the town of Mechanicsville. Towards Beaver Dam Creek, Union troops were entrenched and supported by artillery.

Gen Field's brigade charged across Meadow Bridge sweeping Union pickets through the town of Mechanicsville towards the creek. Gen A. P. Hill gathered his entire division of some 11,000 men to attack the trenched Union forces on the north bank of Beaver Dam Creek.

As the men of the 47th Virginia stood in battle ranks poised for the attack, David prays, "Please Lord keep my family and friends safe this day."

Aaron remarks, "It looks like we have to march over about a mile of open country."

Clay complains, "The Yanks are dug in on the other side of the creek!"

The battle ranks pushed forward into the jaws of chaos. Union artillery opened up with a fury.

Gus yells, "Sweet Jesus, shells are exploding everywhere!"

Just then, a shell explodes in the ranks in front of the 47th and the 40th Virginia Regiments. Dirt, shrapnel, and clothing go flying through the air creating a hole in the ranks. The men step over the dead and wounded as the men try to close ranks. Another shell explodes to the right, and Clay watches a musket catapulting through the air, and sees Pvt George English hit in the thigh by shrapnel.

Company I fires another volley and reloads.

Abner thinks, "The shells pierce the air with a high pitched scream. Oh God! I'm hit! Help me!"

Abner grabs his face as blood covers his hand.

Micah drops next to him, takes a look, and shouts, "Something cut your cheek right smart. Take this scarf and put pressure on it to stop the bleeding."

Joe shouts, "They must have 200 cannons shooting at us. We got to git out of here!"

Clay looks at Joe and shouts, "We don't run like cowards! You have a big mouth! Isn't killing fun anymore, big man?"

Joe fires back, "Shut up!"

Clay shoots back, "You hide behind your big mouth!"

The lieutenant yells, "Keep moving forward!"

The division pushes forward firing volley after volley. Shells continue to explode in the ranks wounding and killing more men. As the division nears the creek, the men go to the ground and shield themselves with anything they can find including the dead. The two sides fire at each other until dark and sleep with their weapons where they are.

Meanwhile, Gen Jackson's troops didn't arrive until late afternoon. Even though he could hear the sounds of battle, he had his men camp, because he didn't know where Gen A. P. Hill and Gen D. H. Hill were.

When Gen McClellan was informed Gen Stonewall Jackson was near his flank, McClellan ordered the V Corps to pull back to Boatswain's Swamp. He was convinced the Rebels were going to capture his supply base at White House Landing and the Richmond and York River Railroad. He had to move his supply base to the James River and move further south away from the Chickahominy River.

The 47th Virginia lost the following men either killed or mortally wounded: Pvt Thomas Burruss Co. K, Pvt Rufus Ennis Co. G, and Pvt John Griffin Co. B at Mechanicsville.

The Union V Corps set up defensive lines on a plateau near Gaines's Mill.

On June 27th, Gen Hill's division marched towards Gaines's Mill that morning. The division reached the swampy terrain around 1:00 pm. Brigades commanded by Generals Gregg, Pender, Anderson, Field, and Branch are ordered to attack the Union position.

Gen Anderson put his brigade on the left side of the road, and Gen Field took the right side. The orders were given to advance.

The 47th Virginia pushed through the difficult terrain in battle ranks towards the plateau. It was difficult to hold their lines. They were attacking to the southwest of Turkey Hill. Gen James Archer's brigade was in front of Field's brigade. Gen Joseph Anderson's brigade was moving in behind Field's brigade.

David thinks, "Is it my time to die? Please protect Aaron and me. Armies shouldn't fight in the bogs and swamps."

Aaron hears artillery coming to life firing shells into the battle ranks. The exploding shells cause holes in the lines, and the men struggle to dress their lines. The brigade and the 47 Virginia position themselves and fire a volley. The brigade in front fires a volley and reloads.

Clay thinks, "Did I hit anyone? Steady yourself and reload. My hands are wet. Don't drop your musket. Lord, my eyes burn."

Micah thinks, "I must hold my ground. Don't panic!"

Suddenly, a soldier drops next to Abner.

He thinks, "Sweet Jesus, he's shot in the eye!"

Joe stumbles over a soldier and cusses. Gus has his canteen shot off his hip.

Clay shouts, "There's so much smoke I can't see nothing!"

David's head pounds from the screech of artillery shells, the roar of explosions, the screams of the wounded, and the hiss of passing bullets. He sees the captain shouting orders, but he can't hear him.

The ranks keep pushing forward stepping over more dead and wounded. Within a 100 yards of the enemy's line, the murderous hail of bullets rip through the ranks. If they stay there without reinforcements, the ranks will die. Every brigade is taking a beating. The order is given to fall back to the tree line. The men pick up as many of the wounded as they can.

When Gen Longstreet came up southwest of Gen A. P. Hill and saw the terrain, he wouldn't attack until Gen Jackson showed up. Once Gen Jackson finally arrived, he met with Gen Lee, so they could put together a plan to attack by 7:00 pm.

When the attack got under way, over 30,000 Confederate soldiers charged along a two mile front. Finally, at dusk the Confederates broke through Union lines in the center and right.

Union Gen Porter withdrew his corps in the early morning hours of June 28th across the Chickahominy River. Gen McClellan ordered his army to retreat to the James River giving up on his campaign.

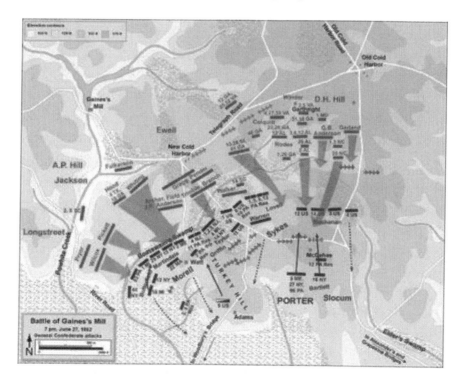

Union casualties from the Battle of Gaines's Mill

totaled almost 7,000 men. Confederate casualties came to almost 8,000 men. The 47th Virginia suffered 34 casualties.

During the Battles of Gaines's Mill, Frayser's Farm and Malvern Hill, the 47th Virginia suffered the following men killed or mortally wounded:

Pvt Dandridge Deatley
Pvt Robert Garrison
Pvt Joseph Mardus
Pvt Henry Patton
Pvt William Sandford
Pvt George Farrar
Pvt Thomas Reynolds
Pvt David Sterne
Capt William Ward
Pvt Andrew Wood
Pvt Mordecai Taylor
Pvt George West

Two brothers named Frank and Warren Sisson were both wounded in the leg at Frayser's Farm and had to be discharged.

Face of the Civil War

Gen Field's and Gen Anderson's brigades, including the 47th Virginia, stayed at Gaines's Mill through June 28th to help recover the wounded and bury the decaying dead. The smell on the battlefield was overpowering, so the men wrapped whatever they could find over their noses.

Joe complains, "All we do is dig trenches and holes to bury the dead."

Pvt Walter Heflin responds, "All you do is complain.

Those trenches give you some protection from enemy fire."

Pvt Patton adds, "We have to bury the dead to cut down on the smell."

Pvt Washington went on, "Lord, the sun has baked the dead black. These darn beetles are everywhere. They feast on the dead."

David asks, "Wasn't it nice of the Yanks to leave their dead behind for us to bury?"

Clay comments, "At least, we took what we needed from the dead."

Gus slaps at a mosquito and says, "Well, this dead mosquito isn't worth burying!"

The men laugh and continue their gruesome task.

Aaron remarks, "I found a good pair of shoes and extra socks courtesy of the Union army."

Micah adds, "Me, too! I even found a new pair of drawers!"

David teases, "I'm real glad, because yours stink some kind of bad!"

Micah fires back, "Well, yours don't smell like flowers."

Gus chimes in, "We all have been stinking ever since we started marching to Richmond."

Pvt Payne saw a snake and started beating it with his shovel. After several strikes, he shouts, "I hate snakes!"

Joe blabs, "You can stop beating it to death, because it was dead two hours ago."

Cpl Embrey suggests, "Let's take a break and go through all these knapsacks the Yanks left behind."

Pvt Thomas Heflin comments, "You can bet we'll find all kinds of things from clothes to food."

David went through one knapsack and found hardtack, a comb, drawers, and a letter. When he read it, tears rolled down his cheeks. It was a letter from the soldier's wife telling him he was a father of a baby girl. All David could do was think about his dear wife and son. He wonders if he will ever see them, again.

Once the Union army started retreating south of the Chickahominy River towards the James River, Gen Lee planned to pitch into them near White Oak Swamp and Glendale.

On June 29th and June 30th, the 47th Virginia marched 20 miles down the Darbytown Road. Gen A. P. Hill's division was ordered to capture or destroy two Yankee batteries pinning down part of the Rebel line.

Gen Field's brigade, including the 47th Virginia, attacked down the Long Bridge Road and rolled up the Union artillery and supporting infantry.

Aaron yells, "We've got them on the run!"

Pvt Powhatan Jones is shot in the right eye and thigh. He crumbles to the ground in agony. Pvt Bennett Woodward is shot in the foot and falls to the ground. Col Robert Mayo is wounded in the arm. Pvt John West falls to the ground wounded. Pvt William West drops in the dirt wounded.

Clay yells, "Turn the guns and fire on them. Load the cannon, Gus!"

The 47th Virginia boys turned the batteries around and poured shell after shell into the retreating Union troops.

Joe yells, "Look at them Yanks skedaddle!"

Abner yells, "The guns are ours, now!"

When darkness descended on the battlefield, the guns fell silent , and the brigade slept with their arms while the Union army retreated to Malvern Hill.

The following day, Gen Field's brigade and Gen A. P. Hill's division were held in reserve. The men thanked God they weren't subjected to the horrific carnage at the Battle of Malvern Hill.

The 47th Virginia and the Light Division returned to within two miles of Richmond and camped at Laurel Hill to recuperate from near exhaustion. The regiment was 1,000 men strong when they arrived in Richmond from Stafford County, Virginia. At the Battle of Glendale, only 156 men were fit for duty. So many were ill with several diseases such as typhoid, diarrhea, dysentery, and fevers. Others were recovering from wounds received during the campaign. The Confederate medical corps had a monumental task to perform with limited medical supplies.

Many patients could have been saved with proper medical care over the long, bitter months of war.

Face of the Civil War

CHAPTER 3

Judge Arthur Murphy's family gathered around the dinner table one evening in June, 1862. He was so proud of the women folk and Teddy. Grace, Kathleen, and Deidre got along well together. Everybody knew they all had to work together during this time of strife.

The family was starting to notice the mercantile store was charging higher prices, and some items were in short supply. Everybody had to cut back on things like sugar, salt, coffee, tea, and spices. Shoes, leather goods, and some materials were getting harder to find.

Thank heavens, Arthur had stocked up on a lot of goods. All the ladies had plenty of material to make clothes. Thanks to his brother, Homer, they had extra foods stored.

Arthur blessed the food, and the family enjoyed the meal together.

Little Andy was walking and talking some foreign language no one understood.

Grace asked, "Any word from Richmond, Poppa?"

"Gen McClellan has retreated to Harrison Landing on the James River."

Kathleen commented, "I hope Gen Lee runs the Union army all the way back to Washington."

Deidre asked, "There's Yankees across the river in Falmouth. Are they going to attack us?"

Arthur answered, "I don't know, but we have troops around to protect us."

Teddy chimed in, "I saw some Yankees taking a bath in the river. Some are fishing, too."

Grace teased, "Yankees have to bathe just like us, Teddy."

"I know, but I'm afraid the Yankees will bust our door down and shoot us!"

Arthur added, "I won't let that happen, son, so don't be afraid."

Kathleen mentioned, "We haven't gotten any letters since our men left for Richmond."

Arthur suggested, "I imagine the boys are busy fighting, and the mail is quite slow."

Deidre remarked, "I hope they have enough food to eat in the army."

Grace continued, "Bless Mr. Amos and Ms. Hattie for bringing us some food and meat from the Wilderness."

Arthur replied, "The boys loved working for Mr. Amos. They are good folks. I'm going hunting with Mr. Amos this weekend."

Kathleen commented, "Fresh venison sure would taste good."

Teddy piped in, "I'm going fishing with Luther after we check his trap lines."

Deidre remarked, "A mess of fried fish would be mighty tasty, too."

Homer and Ellen sat on their front porch wondering where Clay and Gus were. They hadn't gotten mail from them since they left for Richmond. The news from the Peninsula was good, because the Union army was retreating down the James River.

Homer commented, "Gen Lee ran the Yanks right into the river, so that means Richmond is safe."

Ellen added, "Maybe, the boys will be coming back this way."

Homer wondered, "Who knows, our army might attack Washington this time and capture Lincoln."

Ellen went on, "Then, the Yankees will have to

surrender and let us be."

Leann washed her long hair and asked her mother to comb it out for her.

She asked, "Where are the boys?"

Ellen answered, "Ty is putting the chickens to bed, and Harry is saying goodnight to the cows."

Homer laughed and remarked, "That crazy boy likes to say goodnight to the cows. He says they produce sweeter milk when he talks to them."

Leann laughed and added, "Oh Poppa, you know Harry has a gentle spirit."

About that time, Ty stomped up to the porch and fussed, "I told our lazy chickens to lay more eggs!"

Leann teased, "Ty, you need to sweet talk the chickens. Let them know you love them."

"I don't love chickens!"

Ty whirled around and stomped back to the chickens. He walked around the coops, put his hands on his hips, and ordered, "I like you chickens. Now, get busy on those eggs."

When he got back to the porch, Leann asked, "Did you tell the chickens you love them?"

"I told them I liked them. That's all they need to know."

Ellen suggested, "Let's see what happens the next few days."

Ty fussed, "I only love chickens when I'm eating them!"

Harry walked up to the porch from the barn and heard Ty fussing about the chickens.

He asked, "You mean I have to sweet talk the cows to

get more milk?"

Leann responded, "Of course you do! They want to feel your love."

Harry fired back, "The only thing they need to feel is my hands pulling on their tits!"

Leann asked, "Don't you sweet talk the horses all the time?"

Ty shot back, "That's different! Horses are smarter!"

Leann looked at her mother and said, "Men don't git it."

Ellen giggled and replied, "You are so right."

Harry suggested, "I guess you want Ty and me to sweet talk the fish tomorrow when we drop our poles in the river."

Leann answered, "Of course!"

Ty looked at Harry and blabbed, "I ain't sweet talking no fish, ya'll!"

Harry fired back, "Me neither! Besides, fish can't hear."

Ty suggested, "Next thing you know, they'll want us to sweet talk the mosquitoes! Let's git away from these crazy women!"

As the boys headed to the well to draw water, Harry thought, "I can sweet talk when Ty ain't around."

Homer looked at his daughter and commented, "You sure do know how to git your brothers all riled up. You are just what they need."

Ellen added, "One thing for sure, there's never a dull moment around here."

Homer continued, "We have a lot to be thankful for. The crops look good, our trap lines are full, there's plenty of fish in the river, and the woods are full of game."

Leann added, "All of us are in good health, too."
Ellen went on, "Maybe, we'll see the boys soon."
"I pray so, Mama."

As the 47th Virginia rested at Laurel Hill, more men from Company I fell ill or died. Lt William Stewart was admitted to the hospital. Lt James Waple was sent to the hospital in Richmond with consumption. On June 28th, Pvt George West.

Around July 27th, Gen A. P. Hill's Light Division was assigned to Gen Stonewall Jackson. The 47th Virginia remained in Gen Charles Field's Brigade. The 47th Virginia numbered 350 men after getting back several of their sick and slightly wounded. The Light Division boarded a train in Richmond on July 29th and stopped in Gordonsville that evening. The exhausted men slept in the woods near the train.

Gen Lee sent Gen Jackson to stop any Union advance made by Union Gen John Pope. Union troops were positioned in an arc from Sperryville to Little Washington to Falmouth. With Gen Hill's Light Division added to Gen Jackson, his forces numbered around 24,000 men.

David noticed Joe was acting strange, so he went over to check on him.

Joe looked at David and said, "I'm so hot and have diarrhea. I feel really bad."

David felt his head and said, "Good Lord Joe, you're burning up with fever, and it's not from the heat!"

Joe whispered, "I can't walk, David. I'm so weak."

David and Aaron carried Joe to the hospital tent, and an orderly put Joe on a cot. The doctor examined Joe and told his friends he had typhoid.

Joe whispered, "I'm sorry for a lot of things I said and did. If something happens to me, give Teddy my knife and my folks my bible. Killing ain't fun."

Two days later, Pvt Joseph Bishop died. By August 5th, Lt James Waple died from consumption, Pvt Andrew Musselman died from typhoid, Pvt Jonas Jones died from typhoid, and Pvt Travis Dent died from typhoid. Also during July, the company lost another man to desertion.

To draw Confederate forces away from the Peninsula, Gen Pope marched southward into Culpeper County to capture the important rail station at Gordonsville on August 6th.

When Gen Jackson learned only one Union corps was located eight miles south of Culpeper by a creek called Cedar Run, he decided to attack.

The general ordered his army to march to Culpeper on August 7th. Once again, Gen Field's Brigade was ordered to be the rear guard, so they didn't leave Gordonsville until late that evening.

On August 8th, the men marched along the Culpeper-Orange Turnpike.

Clay complains, "Sweet Jesus, it's hot! It must be 100 degrees. How many miles does Gen Jackson want us to march today?"

David answers, "There's no way we can reach Culpeper today! It's 26 miles from Gordonsville!"

Micah remarks, "Thank the Lord Gen Field lets us stop often to drink and rest, because this heat is brutal."

Gus adds, "My uniform is wet and sweat is running

into my shoes."

Aaron states, "When we reach the Rapidan River, I'm jumping in and drink my share of water."

Pvt Brenton teases, "Save some water for us."

The brigade slowed down to pick up men who had dropped out of the ranks from the heat. Both Privates James Bloxton and William Bloxton grabbed a straggler to help him keep up with marching army. Pvt William Patterson helped another soldier who was having terrible leg cramps.

Abner comments, "There are so many men from the front regiments that have dropped on the road."

Clay complains, "I'm tired of eating everybody's dust! It's caked on my face and uniform."

David adds, "We sure do look like ghost troops plastered in red clay, now."

Gen Jackson's lead division only marched eight miles by late evening on August 8th. There was confusion among the orders from Gen Jackson's staff given to the divisional commanders concerning the route they were supposed to take. Also, the intense heat made it necessary to stop more often to rest the men.

The Confederate army crossed the Rapidan River in the morning of August 9th into Culpeper County. Around noon, Gen Jubal Early's lead brigade encountered Union cavalry and artillery seven miles south of Culpeper Court House set up on a ridge above Cedar Run. The battle started as an artillery duel. Both sides charged and counterattacked during the day. The 47th Virginia didn't get to the battlefield until late in the day, and the men were suffering from the heat, dust, and exhaustion.

While foraging around for food, Pvt Steptoe Washington found something he thought the fellers could use.

Steptoe shouted, "Look what I found boys! Whiskey! Pass it around to wash the dust down."

Gus grabbed a bottle and said, "Bless you, Bigtoe, this is just what we need."

The men of Gen Field's Brigade answered the orders to attack the retreating Union troops on Culpeper Court House Road. After chasing the Yankees for about a mile, the brigade pulled back to enjoy the food, supplies, and equipment left behind by the Union army. Fighting on the battlefield stopped around 10:00 pm.

The next morning, Gen Jackson's troops stayed in their positions south of Cedar Mountain waiting for the Union army to attack. Instead, Union troops were allowed to recover their wounded and bury their dead under a flag of truce. Because of the intense heat, burying the dead was extremely difficult.

The 47th Virginia had to help bury the Confederate dead and remove the wounded from the battlefield.

Aaron commented, "I hate taking things from our dead."

Gus responded, "They don't need it."

David stated, "If I'm killed, I want ya'll to take what you need."

Clay remarked, "It looks like all of us managed to find better shoes, drawers, and shirts."

Micah commented, "I found a pair of pants with no holes in them."

Abner mentioned, "I'm looking forward to the Yankee food today. Tonight, we can all write letters home after finding all that paper and ink."

Aaron and Micah went over to a dead soldier, so they could bury him.

Aaron jumped back and shouted, "I can't bury him! Half his head is gone! I got to git away before I vomit!"

Micah replied, "I'll do it. You go on."

Micah looked at the dead soldier and said, "May you rest in peace, sir. I'm sorry we have to bury you away from your family in a grave that will be lost to the ages."

He took the man's holster and pistol along with it's ammunition. He found a pocket watch, so he took that, too. Micah felt like a lowdown thief, but war made folks do a lot of things they weren't proud of to stay alive.

Union casualties at the Battle of Cedar Mountain totaled almost 2,400 men while the Confederates lost almost 1,400 men.

On August 11th, Gen Jackson moved his army back to Gordonsville and waited for reinforcements from Gen Lee. Those reinforcements were led by Gen James Longstreet. The two commands totaled about 55,000 men. Gen Lee wanted to defeat Union Gen Pope's army before Gen McClellan could reinforce Gen Pope from the Peninsula.

Before Gen Longstreet's Corps arrived to join Gen Jackson, Company I recorded three more desertions.

On August 16th, Gen Jackson and Gen Longstreet marched their troops to Clark's Mountain.

On August 20th through August 21st, Gen Jackson's troops drove fleeing Union forces back through Stevensburg, Brandy Station, and right up to the Rappahannock River. The Yankees guarded all the fords on the river, because they didn't want Jackson to cross them.

Gen Field's Brigade arrived at Waterloo Bridge on August 25th. The Yankees were trying to burn the bridge, but the brigade poured fire into the Yanks all day.

Gus wiped sweat and asked, "When are the Yankees going to learn they can't torch the bridge, because we keep running them off?"

Clay commented, "I wish they would leave, so we can jump in the river to cool off."

David responded, "I guess the Yanks aren't very smart, and a swim sounds wonderful."

Abner complained, "Lord, it's hot as hades! If I burst into flames, ya'll don't be surprised."

Aaron saw a Union soldier run towards the bridge, so he took careful aim and fired.

He commented, "Lord forgive me. I think I killed him."

Gus responded, "He shouldn't have had a torch."

After dark, the men ate and slept. David dreamed about his wife and son wondering if they were alright. He desperately wanted to hold his wife and child in his arms and never let go. He wanted his life back like it was before the war.

Aaron dreamed about his wonderful wife and wanted to feel her arms hugging him. He prayed they would have children and get their lives back. He wondered how long the war was going to drag on. Would his family remain safe?

Faces of the Civil War

CHAPTER 4

Company I was jolted awake by Sgt Jones around 2:30 am on August 25th at Salem (present-day Marshall).

Sgt Jones ordered, "Get ready and fall into ranks. We're ordered to Manassas Junction to destroy and capture the Yankee supply depot."

David chimed in, "That means food and lots of other things to take for ourselves."

Micah rubbed his sore aching feet and complained, "We marched 26 miles today. If we keep this up, I won't have any feet left. Shoot fire! My shoes are almost gone."

Clay responded, "Resting ten minutes every hour didn't make the heat and dust go away. My uniform is full of dirt."

Gus remarked, "If we keep this up, I'll end up as nothing but a pile of sweating flesh!"

David teased, "We'll make sure we don't step on you."

Gus fired back, "That was mighty nice to say, you crazy fool!"

On August 26th, they had marched 30 miles and hit Bristoe Station on the Orange and Alexandria Railroad. All the men were footsore, hot, and exhausted. At least, they weren't that far from Manassas. All of them wanted to get their hands on the food and destroy the railroad.

By daylight on August 27th, they had marched to Manassas Junction and defeated the Union troops in the area. The men couldn't believe their eyes when they looked upon the piles of food, clothing, and supplies left behind.

The Confederate soldiers went about eating their fill, taking badly needed clothes, and anything else they needed. What they couldn't carry was destroyed. In this case, the Quartermaster Corps hadn't made plans to take the leftover food and supplies.

Gen Jackson marched his army to Centreville during the night of August 27th through August 28th north of the First Manassas battlefield. They spread out in defensive positions behind an unfinished railroad grade in heavy woods that concealed them. Gen Hill's brigades were behind the railroad cut near Sudley Church.

On August 30th, the brigade was ordered to support the center of the Confederate line, because the Louisianans were throwing rocks at the enemy having run out of ammunition. When the brigade arrived, they fired a volley into the Union ranks and attacked.

David yells, "The Yankee line is retreating!"

Sgt Jones orders, "Pour fire into them boys! Don't stop, boys, keep after them!"

Clay yells, "The whole brigade has the Yanks on the run!"

Micah had a retreating Yank in his sights and pulled the trigger.

He prays, "Please forgive me for shooting a man in the back."

Aaron aimed his musket and sighted a Union drummer boy. He slid his aim to the right and fired, instead.

He thought, "I will not shoot a drummer boy!"

The brigade was like a wave crashing onto the beach.

The second Union line collapsed and retreated into the woods.

The order came for the brigade to get back to the railroad cut and relieve the Louisiana Brigade, so they could get badly needed ammunition.

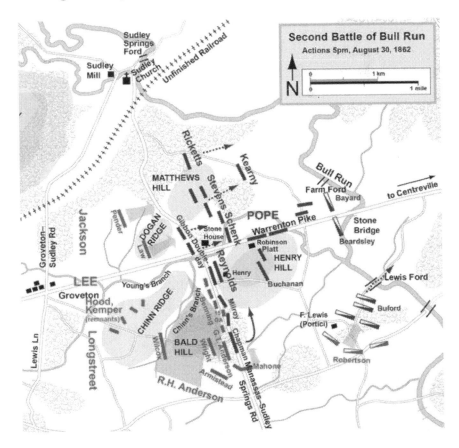

In a driving rainstorm, Col Brockenbrough's Brigade led the chase of the Yankee army down the Little River Turnpike and through the town of Chantilly to Fairfax Courthouse on August 31st.

A violent thunderstorm and darkness put an end to the fighting between the two exhausted opposing armies on September 1st.

The following day, the Union army retreated to Washington, D. C. Obviously, the defeat at Second Manassas was a blow to Union morale. President Lincoln had no other choice but to relieve Gen Pope from command.

Union casualties were around 10,000 killed and wounded at the Second Battle of Manassas. The Confederate army lost 8,300 killed and wounded.

The following men from the 47th Virginia were killed or mortally wounded during the Battle of 2nd Manassas:

Pvt James Ball	Pvt Beckwith Barker
Pvt George Coates	Pvt William Jackson
Pvt James Kelley	Pvt Mordecai Lawson
Pvt Henry Loving	Pvt Charles Powers
Pvt Richard Saunders	Pvt George Delany

The men learned from Chaplain Meredith that Pvt Thomas Cooper and Pvt Alexander Dent died from typhoid. During August, Company I lost three more men to desertion.

The Confederate army started marching towards Maryland by September 3rd. Col Brockenbrough's Brigade arrived in Leesburg on September 4th and the Potomac River by September 5th. The brigade rested in Frederick, Maryland until September 10th.

Gen Jackson's Corps was ordered to capture Harper's Ferry, so Gen Jackson decided to let his artillery loose on the Union garrison from the heights. The artillery battle was quickly over when the garrison surrendered.

Gen Hill's Light Division enjoyed the captured Union supplies and food. Some of the men even grabbed new

Union uniforms, because theirs were worn out, full of holes, and filthy. At the Battle of Antietam, these uniforms would cause confusion on the battlefield. Most of the friends grabbed new trousers even though they were light blue.

Gen Lee sent word to Gen Jackson on the morning of September 17th to march to Sharpsburg as quickly as possible. Gen Hill's Division marched the 17 miles in less than eight hours. The Union army had no idea 3,000 new Rebel troops had reinforced the Rebel right.

Gen Hill put Gen Pender's and Col Brockenbrough's Brigades on the right at the end of the line. Gen Hill ordered Gen Gregg's Brigade of South Carolina boys to attack. They charged into farmer John Otto's cornfield routing the newly formed 16th Connecticut. The 4th Rhode Island got confused by the southern boys wearing Yankee uniforms, and their line collapsed and retreated. The 8th Connecticut was driven out of the cornfield and down the hills by Antietam Creek.

After Gen Hill's successful counterattack, he ordered Col Brockenbrough's Brigade to protect the Snavely Ford on the Antietam River.

Aaron commented, "I'm so tired I can hardly walk. If I fall asleep walking, please pick me up before somebody stomps on me."

David replied, "Don't worry, I'll help you along."

Clay asked, "Haven't we marched enough this summer to get to California?"

Pvt Thomas Brewer answered, "It sure seems like it. At least, today ain't 100 degrees."

Gus continued, "I'm glad we didn't have to charge into

that cornfield. I guess that makes me a coward for thinking that way."

Micah fired back, "No, it don't! We've been in our share of nasty fights!"

Abner remarked, "The sergeant warned us about eating green corn, but just look at all the fools running to the bushes with dia-ree."

Just then, Aaron slumped to the ground fast asleep. David picked him up in his arms and kept walking.

Pvt Steptoe Washington chimed in, "I thought invading Maryland would provide us with more food. In my opinion, the Quartermaster Corps needs to be kicked into the Potomac River. I'm tired of being hungry most of the time, ya'll!"

Micah responded, "I agree, Big Toe!"

Pvt Washington shot back, "It's a good thing we're friends, or I'd kick you in the river if I had the strength."

Pvt Thomas West added, "I'm dead on my dead feet."

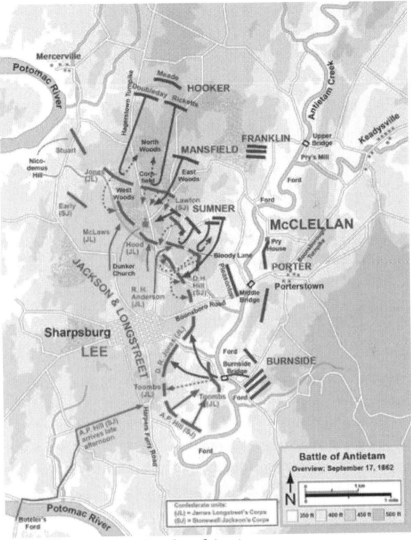

Battle of Antietam

Antietam cornfield

The men reached Snavely Ford and collapsed, too exhausted to cook their meager rations.

Late the following day, Gen Lee withdrew his army and crossed back into Virginia on September 19th. The Light Division attacked the pursuing Union troops near Boteler's Ford and pushed the Yankee forces back into Maryland.

Gen Jackson's Corps set up in Winchester until October 16th. The men desperately needed rest, food, and re-supply. For a short while, Col Brockenbrough's Brigade tore up railroad tracks between Harper's Ferry and Martinsburg. In early November, the brigade performed picket duty on the Shenandoah River at Snicker's Ford.

Lincoln relieved Gen George McClellan when he didn't destroy Gen Lee's army after the Battle of Antietam. He was replaced by Gen Ambrose Burnside. His plan was to go through Fredericksburg to get to Richmond. In order to do that, he needed pontoon bridges to cross the Rappahannock River. As fate would have it, Gen Burnside couldn't get the pontoons to Falmouth before Gen Lee moved his army to block him.

Gen Longstreet's Corps arrived first on November 23rd. Lee placed them on Marye's Heights, behind the town, to the west of town on Snowden Hill, and east of the town behind the Richmond, Fredericksburg, and Potomac Railroad tracks.

Gen Lee sent for Gen Stonewall Jackson's Corps on November 26th. However, Gen Jackson sensed Lee would need him, so he force-marched his men starting on November 22nd from Winchester. The corps averaged just under 20 miles a day.

Col Brockenbrough's Brigade didn't need to be pushed, because they were heading home to protect their families. The boys from Stafford County were worried about the Union troop buildup in their county. The boys from south of the Rappahannock River didn't want Yankees in their counties and homes. All hoped they could see their loved ones before the Yankees attacked.

David and Aaron wondered if their father was still in Fredericksburg, or had he moved in with their Uncle Homer in Caroline County.

Gen Jackson's men marched down the Shenandoah Valley, crossed the Blue Ridge Mountains, marched through Orange Court House, and arrived at Gen Lee's headquarters on November 29th.

Gen Lee sent Jackson's Corps east of Fredericksburg to prevent a downstream crossing by Union forces.

Gen A. P. Hill's Light Division was sent six miles southeast of town near Hamilton's Crossing and Prospect Hill. From Prospect Hill, the men had a clear view of the Rappahannock River and the Richmond, Fredericksburg, and Potomac Railroad. The 47th and 22nd Virginia regiments were placed at the foot of the hill and told to dig trenches and fortify them. The 40th and 55th Virginia regiments along with the artillery set up on the top of Prospect Hill.

Jackson's other divisions set up at Port Royal, Skinker's Neck, and along the railroad near Guinea Station.

Fredericksburg Campaign

Sgt Embrey suggested, "Alright men, let's dig this ditch deeper, so we have more room. Then, pile whatever you can find in front of us for protection."

Pvt Anderson asked, "Can we cut down some trees, Sergeant?"

He answered, "Sure, just don't let it fall on your head."

David laughed and teased, "Don't worry, Sergeant, we'll yell *timber*, but Anderson's head will split that tree plum in two."

Pvt Anderson shot back, "My head ain't that hard. I should kick your behind, David."

Aaron teased, "Don't do that, because his behind is hard enough to break your foot!"

Pvt Ball asked, "Sergeant, can we make a quick visit home to check on our families?"

The sergeant answered, "You fellers from Stafford County can't go, because there's Yankees everywhere. There must be 100,000 Yankees over there. You try to see your families, and the Yankees will capture your behinds. For the rest of you, we need every man on the line, because we don't know when the Yankees are going to attack. When we beat the pants off the Yanks, then, we can think about checking on our loved ones."

David suggested, "The Yanks are up to something, because they're mighty busy over there."

Clay added, "They must have 200 cannons set up on the Stafford Heights."

Gus remarked, "I bet some Union general has his headquarters in Chatham Manor."

Aaron chimed in, "I love that beautiful home and the property. That's some fine living up there."

Micah commented, "I hope the Yankees don't destroy the home. The Lacy House is a special home. It shouldn't be destroyed."

David mentioned, "I don't know if Poppa is still in Fredericksburg, or if he's taken our families to Uncle Homer's place."

Clay replied, "I hope they're with Homer and mother."

Abner added, "My house is west of the town near Snowden Hill. Yankee artillery could kill my folks."

Sgt Embrey replied, "Don't borrow trouble. We'll pitch into the Yankees before they hurt our families."

On December 6th, Judge Murphy talked with the doctor. Deidre and Teddy were sick with bad colds and coughing a lot. Arthur wanted to move his family to Homer's farm, but he felt it was too dangerous.

The doctor informed Arthur, "You can't move Deidre and Teddy in these freezing temperatures. Both of them will end up with pneumonia."

Arthur responded, "I was afraid of that. Are they any better?"

The doctor answered, "Yes, as long as they stay warm and take this medicine for their coughs."

Arthur replied, "Little Andy is doing fine, now, after you treated him, so I'll make sure they follow your orders."

The doctor mentioned, "The Yankee buildup across the river is worrying me, Arthur."

"Me too. However, my family will defend our home. All the women folk know how to shoot a gun. We'll barricade ourselves in the house and shoot to kill."

"Have you heard from the boys?"

Arthur responded, "A Mississippi soldier brought us three letters from David, Aaron, and Micah. The 47th Virginia is around Prospect Hill. None of the men can check on their families. Somehow, the boys got the letters through letting us know they're near and ready for battle."

"Didn't Micah's parents close up their home and move in with his sister in Lancaster County?"

"Yes, but Micah doesn't know that. Abner's family is still here. At least, they live further west from town than us."

The doctor continued, "Everywhere you look along Stafford Heights there are artillery batteries and tents. When the Yankees start firing their cannons, it won't be long before the infantry will cross the river."

Arthur mentioned, "Our home is well stocked with food, water, and firewood. If we need to, we can barricade the doors and windows. What worries me the most are artillery shells hitting my home. Exploding shells could kill or injure my family, start fires, and destroy our town."

The doctor added, "If there's fighting in the streets, innocent civilians are going to be in the middle of two raging armies with no place to hide."

Arthur responded, "This is a new kind of war. We have to do everything possible to stay alive."

The friends talked for a while longer, and then said their goodbyes.

Early on December 11th, Yankee engineers started putting together six pontoon bridges across the Rappahannock River. Engineers directly in front of the town were being killed or wounded by sharpshooters in the buildings of the town. One hundred and fifty cannons bombarded the town, but they weren't able to stop the sharpshooters deadly fire.

In the afternoon, the 7th Michigan, 19th

Massachusetts, and 20th Massachusetts crossed the river and went through the streets searching for the enemy.

The Union batteries fired over 5,000 shells at the town by nightfall. Several Union brigades proceeded to loot Fredericksburg with a vengeance. Furniture, portraits, and much more were tossed in the streets and destroyed or stolen. Artillery shells damaged homes and started fires.

Looting & burning of Fredericksburg

Looting & burning of Fredericksburg

Little Andy was walking towards his mother when an artillery shell screamed overhead and exploded about eighty yards away. Andy burst into tears, yelled, and ran into his mother's arms.

Kathleen held her terrified, crying child and tried to comfort him.

She said, "Don't cry Andy, that boom was far away. We won't let it hurt you."

Arthur asked, "Are all the shutters closed over the windows?"

Grace answered, "Yes, Poppa."

Another shell exploded a little closer, and the house rattled and shook.

Teddy ran to his father and asked, "Why are they shooting at us?"

Arthur answered, "They're shooting at our soldiers, but some of the shells are landing in the wrong places."

Teddy shouted, "Make it stop, Poppa! It makes me scared! The Yankees are shooting at David and Aaron!"

"Our army is fighting back, Teddy. Gen Lee will beat the Yankees. The boys will run the Yanks back across the river."

Teddy asked, "You promise, Poppa."

"The boys and I won't let anybody hurt you."

Teddy asked, "What's that cracking noise?"

Arthur held his son and answered, "It's musket fire. The Mississippi sharpshooters are shooting at the Yankees. Teddy, you're not well yet, so lie down on the sofa and wrap up nice and warm."

The family decided to stay in the living room and dining room, so they could stay warmer near the large fireplace. Arthur knew he could protect his family better when they were near.

After dinner, the women folk made pallets on the floor for everyone to sleep on. Deidre and Teddy would sleep on the sofas, because they were still recovering.

Arthur brought more firewood inside from the back porch. He looked towards the town east of him and saw the orange glow from the fires burning. He thought they must have started from the exploding shells.

He wondered, "I wish I knew what is going on. I have no idea which side is winning. How long will the battle last? Will my sons and family be safe?"

On December 12th, Union soldiers crossed the river in large numbers. As fate would have it, vague orders, incorrect maps, and conservative generals bogged down Union movements for most of the day.

December 13th was overcast and very cold. There was a thick fog that covered the ground, and the fog looked like ghosts sweeping through the streets of Fredericksburg.

Union Gen William Franklin expected orders to attack south of the city by his entire Grand Division of about 60,000 men. Instead, he was ordered to send no less than a division to attack Prospect Hill around Hamilton's Crossing. Gen George Meade's division of 4,500 men was chosen to mount the attack supported by Gen John Gibbon's division.

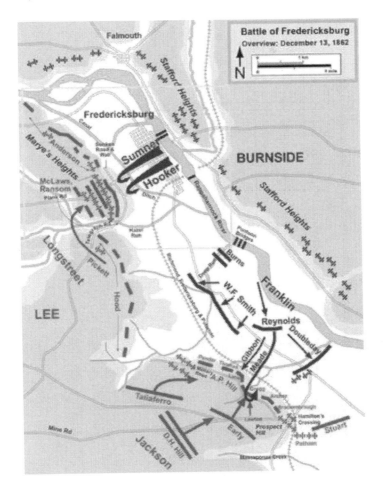

They started marching along the river around 8:30 am. When they turned right towards Richmond Road, Gen Jeb Stuart's Horse Artillery started pounding their positions. When the fog lifted around 10:30 am, Gen Jackson's batteries started firing at Gen Meade's division. Gen Meade was frustrated, because his movements were stopped about 600 yards from Prospect Hill. Around 1:00 pm, the Union artillery stopped firing, and the Union division moved forward.

Gen Ambrose Burnside   Gen William Franklin

Gen John Gibbon   Gen James Lane

Gen James Archer   Gen Jubal Early

David whispered, "Hold your fire until they git real close."

Aaron thinks, "They can't see us concealed behind our fortifications."

Micah thinks, "Easy, easy! Wait for the order to fire!"

The captain yells, "Fire!"

The men of the 47th and 22nd Virginia poured volley after volley into the devastated Union lines forcing them to move further to their right. This forced them into a dense swampy thicket between Gen Archer's and Gen Lane's Brigades. This 600 yard gap between the Confederate generals gave Gen Meade's men the opportunity to roll up the Rebel flanks.

The 47th Virginia and the 22nd Virginia Battalion were rapidly moved behind Prospect Hill to help plug the gap. Between Gen Gregg's brigade and men from Generals Jubal Early and William Taliaferro, the Confederates rallied and beat back the Union forces. Eventually, the Union troops moved back to the river even though both sides kept firing at each other until sundown.

Gen David Gregg   Gen William Taliaferro

Meanwhile, in front of Marye's Heights along a stone wall, seven Union divisions bashed themselves against the wall in 14 different charges, but couldn't break the Confederate lines. That carnage cost the Union between 6,000 to 8,000 casualties.

Stonewall at Fredericksburg

Stonewall at Fredericksburg

Clay looked at Gus and said, "We held the end of the line and filled the air with bullets when the Yanks attacked."

Gus replied, "Our regiment did good. I wonder what's happening in town and on the left."

Abner added, "There was a lot of battle noise from the town."

Micah mentioned, "I'm worried to death about my parents in town. I pray my home is still standing, and my parents are safe. The not knowing is driving me crazy!"

Abner added, "I'm scared, too. My folks have to be alright!"

David remarked, "I'm sure we'll get a chance to check on our families when we chase the Yanks across the river."

Aaron continued, "Lord is it cold! I want to be home with my beautiful wife in front of the fireplace kissing her crazy."

Arthur stepped out on his back porch with Grace to bring in more firewood. He looked up at the night sky and was shocked to see the Northern Lights.

Grace asked, "What is that, Poppa? It looks like sheets of different colored lights."

"It's the Aurora Borealis."

"I've never seen such a thing before."

"It's quite rare this far south. Folks in Canada see it often."

"What's that popping sound?"

"I have no idea, Grace. Maybe, it's part of the Aurora Borealis. It could be static electricity making that sound."

"I'm going to get Kathleen and Deidre, so they can see it."

"That's a good idea. I'll get Teddy. Make sure Deidre stays wrapped up in her heavy blanket."

The armies remained in their positions on December 14th. Gen Burnside asked Gen Lee to grant him a truce, so he could recover his wounded where they had fallen. Gen Lee granted the truce and wondered how many men were still alive after the bitter cold temperatures overnight.

Union casualties at the Battle of Fredericksburg totaled 12, 653 men. Confederate casualties numbered 5, 377 men. The Union army saw how disastrous their battle tactics were. Attacking in battle ranks at a well-fortified position on high ground was insane carnage.

The following men from the 47th Virginia were killed during the Battle of Fredericksburg:

Pvt Thomas S. Burruss   Pvt James Busby
Pvt James Carter   Pvt John Cook

Pvt Alexander Coons
Pvt Henry Fones
Pvt William B. Lawson
Pvt James Newsome

Pvt John Cox
Cpl Russell Fones
Pvt Walker Monroe
Pvt John Pritchett

Gen Lee was still irate over the looting of Fredericksburg. He knew his Virginia regiments would never forget what happened here. This was not a gentlemen's war.

On December 15th, Gen Burnside ordered his army back to Falmouth on the north side of the Rappahannock River.

Chatham Manor was indeed used as headquarters for Union Gen Edwin Sumner. Then, it became a hospital with the floors of its 12 rooms covered with wounded Union soldiers. The wounded that died were buried on the plantation property along with the scores of amputated limbs. People such as Clara Barton and Walt Whitman took care of the wounded in Chatham.

Chatham Manor   Fredericksburg Ruins

Faces of the Civil War

Damaged home in Fredericksburg

Damaged home in Fredericksburg

Fredericksburg Baptist Church

CHAPTER 5

On December 17th, Col Brockenbrough's Brigade marched to Port Royal to check out rumors that the Union army had crossed the river, but the rumors were false.

Gen Jackson set up winter quarters at Moss Neck in Caroline County near the James Corbin Mansion. The general refused to stay in the mansion, but he did occupy the office building next to the main residence.

Arthur heard a knock at the front door.

He grabbed his weapon, stood next to the door, and shouted, "Identify yourself!"

David yelled, "It's your sons, Poppa!"

Arthur unlocked the door and threw it open. He had never seen such a wonderful sight. They held onto each other for dear life and wept tears of joy.

Grace heard the commotion and walked into the living room. She shouted their names and ran into her brothers' arms. Arthur shouted for the others to come running.

Teddy ran into the living room, saw the reunion, and launched himself into his brothers. They hugged each other tightly and cried rivers of tears.

Kathleen, Andy, and Deidre rushed into the room and stopped dead in their tracks. It was all Kathleen and Deidre could do to keep from sinking to their knees on the floor like crying fools.

David rushed to his wife and son, took them in his arms, and hugged them tightly. Little Andy kept patting his daddy's face and blabbing some foreign baby language. David and Kathleen wiped each other's tears in between kisses. To David she felt so good and smelled divine. Her hair and skin were so soft.

Aaron rushed to his wife, took her into his arms, and kissed her downright silly. She smelled so fresh and clean compared to him. He was going to take a bath and scrub down good, because he knew he didn't smell like a rose. He was worried about Deidre's cough, but she assured him she and Teddy were much better.

Micah shook Arthur's hand and asked, "Where are my parents, Judge Murphy?"

"They're in Lancaster with your aunt and uncle."

"Thank the Lord, they're safe. Judge, my home is nothing but a shell. My mother's piano is in the backyard beat to pieces. The streets are littered with broken furniture, dishes, pictures, and all kinds of things. The town was looted, but we beat the Yankees back across the river."

Arthur ran his hand through his hair and replied, "That makes me furious! Looters are nothing but common thieves. We knew fires were burning in town, but we didn't know about the looters."

"They were probably looking for sharpshooters and decided to loot while they were at it. One thing for sure, the Yanks will remember Marye's Heights."

Grace asked, "Are you hungry, Micah?"

"I'm starving along with David and Aaron."

She suggested, "Come help me put together a meal for you fellers."

"Sure! I know my way around a kitchen."

When they had some privacy, Micah hugged her close and said, "I have missed you so. Your letters meant the world to me. I'm so glad you are safe."

She went on, "Your letters made me miss you more."

He took a deep breath and commented, "I care for you deeply. Will you wait for me until the war is over?"

She responded with a smile, "If you won't say it, I will. I'll wait for you, because I love you with all my heart."

"You do! I have loved you for a long time, Grace. When the war is over, will you marry me?"

"Of course, I will!"

"Then, I'll speak to your father before we leave."

Before they got started on the meal, he kissed Grace until she thought her shoes were going to blow plum off her feet.

Aaron spoke up and said, "All of us are a mess. We haven't had a bath and shave for quite a while. Please excuse our uniforms, because they're hard to replace."

David added, "We have Yankee pants, drawers, and shoes on. Sometimes, we have to take what we need from the enemy."

Arthur asked, "How long can you stay?"

He answered, "We can stay three days. When we get back to Moss Neck, we have to build huts for our winter quarters. We've named our place Camp Gregg in honor of Gen Gregg who was killed.

Arthur mentioned, "You'll be about ten miles south of us, so we'll bring you food and clothing when it gets warmer."

Aaron responded, "That would be wonderful. Maybe, we can spend Christmas together."

Arthur added, "Grace is fixing you up with a fine meal."

David replied, "Some home cooking will be a blessing."

The boys feasted on chicken, potatoes, cornbread, and warm apple cider. To them, it was a meal fit for a king.

Micah asked, "Where did you get the cider?"

Grace answered, "Mr. Amos brought us quite a bit from his orchard."

David commented, "I miss Amos. He taught us a lot, and he is a good man. I pray his family stays safe."

Aaron teased, "You know, if we sic Ms. Hattie on the Yankees, the war will be over in two days."

Everyone laughed and agreed Ms. Hattie could tie all those Yankees into a knot in no time.

After Kathleen and Grace cleaned up the kitchen, David called Teddy over and said, "Teddy, Joe wanted you to have his knife, so take real good care of it."

"What happened to Joe?"

"He got real sick with typhoid fever and died."

"It's really nice. I'll take good care of it and treat it like a special gift."

Grace chimed in, "It's an early Christmas present."

"That's right! It's the second early Christmas present."

Micah asked, "What do you mean?"

"The first present was seeing the beautiful lights in the sky."

Micah responded, "We saw them, too. They were beautiful, but they scared the bejesus out of some of the Mississippi boys. They thought the lights were evil spirits coming to get them."

Kathleen commented, "Something that beautiful can't be evil. I believe it was a good omen."

David remarked, "It was a good omen, because all of

us are together."

Arthur replied, "Amen to that! I'm going to set up a tub in the coat room leading to the back porch. You fellers can bathe, and I'll cut your hair."

Micah asked, "Do you need more firewood brought in, Judge?"

"Yes, I'd like plenty for all the fireplaces."

Teddy spoke up, "I'll bring down towels, cloths, soap, and nightshirts, Poppa."

"That's good."

When bath time was finished, the boys felt like humans, again. They were clean from head to toe, their hair was cut, and their beards were trimmed. While the fireplaces warmed the rooms, David and Aaron took their wives in their arms and loved them like they had fantasized so many times in their dreams.

Homer heard a knock at his door and grabbed his gun.

He shouted, "Who's there?"

Clay yelled back, "It's your sons, Poppa!"

Homer unlocked the door, threw it open, and hugged his stepsons. Ellen came running from another room and burst into tears when she saw her boys.

Ellen shouted, "The Lord be praised! It's really you!"

The boys hugged their mother as they all wept tears of joy.

Ellen commented, "You boys are so thin. We have to get some food into you."

Leann, Ty, and Harry came running and launched themselves into Clay's and Gus's arms.

Clay commented, "You three have gotten taller since

we last saw you."

Homer teased, "I can see the pant legs crawling up each boy's legs."

Gus remarked, "Leann, you're growing into a fine looking young woman."

Leann fired back, "Gus, you tell that to all the young ladies."

Homer continued, "Ty and Harry are doing a great job on the farm."

Ty jumped in, "I have to sweet talk the chickens, so they'll lay more eggs! I think it's plum stupid!"

Gus teased, "If it works, you better keep it up."

Harry blabbed, "I have to sweet talk the cows and fish. I don't think it works!"

Clay teased, "Every person and animal needs some sweet talking, so keep it up."

Gus asked, "We're starving! Do you have something to eat?"

Leann answered, "I can fix ya'll up with eggs, bacon, potatoes, and biscuits with honey real quick."

Clay suggested, "Cook up plenty, because we want some home cooking!"

Leann and Ellen headed for the kitchen while the fellers caught up on the news. Clay told Homer about the Battle of Fredericksburg and 2nd Manassas. Homer was furious about the looting in the town.

Clay commented, "We're sorry we look so bad and smell like mules, but the last four months have been difficult. We've marched enough to go to China and back."

Homer responded, "Don't worry none. We'll get you all cleaned up and well fed. Ya'll want some coffee?"

Gus shot back, "You bet we do with some milk in it!"

Homer asked, "How long can you stay?"

Gus replied, "We only have three days."

"Then, we'll make the most of it. Why didn't Arthur bring his family here?"

Gus answered, "We don't know. David, Aaron, Abner, and Micah headed to Fredericksburg. We won't know anything until we get back to Moss Neck."

Homer mentioned, "We'll be able to get to you when the weather is good. We'll bring you some home cooking and clothes."

Clay remarked, "Homer, we don't have enough rations, we don't get paid every month, we don't get much mail, and our uniforms are nothin' but rags."

Gus continued, "We steal all kinds of things from the Yankee dead. We wear Yankee overcoats in camp to stay warm. We go through their knapsacks, because we know there's hardtack, candy, paper, ink, drawers, socks, and gloves in a lot of them."

Clay went on, "At first, it bothered us to steal from the dead, but not anymore."

Homer asked, "Why can't you get the clothes and supplies you need?"

Gus answered, "I guess we don't have the resources and manufacturing the Yanks have."

Homer said, "That worries me a lot. If we can't feed our army, how long can we fight? I heard a rumor that the Yanks are blockading the coast and lots of rivers."

Clay mentioned, "They are blockading. We invaded Maryland to collect supplies, livestock, and food. Virginia is being stripped like vultures picking on a carcass."

Homer asked, "How is morale?"

Gus answered, "It's high, because Gen Lee is winning most battles. We still have a lot of deserters. Most of them ain't worth a poop. Lazy cowards get good men killed."

Clay continued, "Homer, disease is killing more men than the fighting."

He commented, "We heard measles, typhoid, and diarrhea is real bad. Do you have enough medicines?"

"No! You'll never know how horrible it is to hear a wounded soldier beg for mercy during an amputation."

Gus added, "Don't tell mother what horrible things we have seen."

"Don't worry, I won't. I'm glad Ty and Harry are getting eggs and milk. They don't need to know this."

Clay stated, "David, Aaron, Abner, and Micah are fine soldiers. We can all trust each other with our lives. If you can't trust the man next to you on the battlefield, you have nothin'."

Homer pondered, "Trust is one of the things people must have between each other. I trust your mother with my life."

Shortly, the boys were called to the table to enjoy a home cooked meal. The fellers ate until they thought they would pop.

Harry teased, "Where did you put all that food?"

Gus shot back, "In our legs!"

Everyone laughed and teased each other. Gus and Clay relished every minute of the fun and laughter. How very special their family was. They wanted the war to end soon, so they could come back to this paradise.

After the meal, Homer helped the fellers scrub weeks of war off of them, so they could feel normal, again. It was so good to be clean and put on nightshirts. Ellen told her sons she'd clean their uniforms up the best she could and sew up the holes and rips.

That first night home, they crawled between the bed covers and laid their heads on soft pillows. Tears gathered in their eyes, because this would only last for two more days.

Abner knocked on his door and was met with his father pointing a pistol at him.

His father burst into tears of joy and shouted, "Thank God you're alive!"

They embraced and wept oceans of tears. Soon, his mother and fifteen year old sister Eva were wrapped around him hugging and crying in his arms.

He looked around the warm living room, but he didn't see his brother, Richard.

He asked, "Where's my brother?"

Walter answered, "Richard took sick in November with pneumonia. The doctor did everything he could for him, but it doesn't look like he's going to get better."

Abner rushed into his brother's room and gathered him in his arms. Richard opened his eyes and smiled.

"You came to see me. I didn't want to die before I could see you, again."

Abner shot back, "You're not going to die, because we have things to do together when the war is over."

"Did we win the battle?"

"We sure did! We beat the Yanks good. Gen Lee chased them back across the river."

"I'm glad. I don't want Yanks in the house."

Abner asked, "Are you warm enough?"

"Yes, and I want some water."

Abner wrapped his brother in a warm blanket and took him in the living room by the fireplace. He held Richard in his arms on the sofa while Luella fetched the water.

Abner asked, "Are you hungry?"

"I'd like to have a biscuit and honey. Are you hungry, Abner?"

"I'm starving! Why don't we eat right here?"

"I'd like that."

Abner's mother fixed a plate for both her sons. Eggs, bacon, and biscuits never tasted so good.

It wasn't long before Richard drifted off to sleep, but Abner refused to lay him down. He wanted to spend as much time as he could with his little brother.

His father asked, "We don't git much mail, so we didn't know if you were here."

"We marched from Winchester and got here before the Yanks crossed the river. Gen Jackson put us on Prospect Hill."

"My heavens! You mean the Yankees attacked that far south of town?"

"Yes, sir!"

Luella commented, "I'm glad the Yanks are on the other side of the river. Did they burn the town?"

"Some buildings burned and were hit by artillery shells."

His sister remarked, "I hope nobody got hurt."

"I don't know about that, but all of us are furious the Yanks looted our town!"

She answered, "We didn't know they were looting!"

"Oh yes! Micah's home was looted and burned."

His sister replied, "That's down right mean! Thank the Lord his parents went to Lancaster."

"I'm very relieved to hear that. Mama, we write letters when we find paper and ink in Yankee knapsacks. None of us have enough money to buy some from the thieving sutlers. They want a $1.25 for a bar of soap."

Walter shouted, "That is disgraceful!"

"We haven't been paid for months. Lord knows if we'll git paid by Christmas."

Eva asked, "Will the army let you come home for Christmas?"

"I don't know, honey. I hope so."

Eva added, "I pray Richard will be well by then."

Luella went on, "He ate more food tonight than he has in several days."

His father added, "Abner, I think you perked him up some."

Abner mentioned, "His cough worries me. He sounds so congested."

His mother commented, "Maybe, coughing up the phlegm helps him."

Abner responded, "If the mucus is bloody, it's not a good thing. When our soldiers were sick with pneumonia in the hospital tents, bloody mucus was a bad sign."

Eva replied, "I haven't seen any blood."

"That's good to hear."

His father suggested, "I'll take Richard, so you can take a warm bath in the mud room."

Abner smiled and responded, "I'm glad that room isn't open to the back porch."

Eva teased, "You'd turn into a block of ice."

Luella went on, "I'll cut your hair and trim your beard. The beard makes you look older and very mature."

Abner smiled and said, "I feel like I'm an old man."

His sister teased, "You look like you're 80 years old."

"Thanks, Sis! I was thinking more like 50 years old."

The bath was like heaven to Abner. He couldn't remember when he last had a bath with a bar of soap. He was embarrassed that he smelled so bad, and his uniform was a mess. He hoped a good scrub, hair washed and cut, and his beard trimmed would kill all the varmints camped out on his body and uniform. He would gladly accept a mended, clean uniform.

That night, he slept in Richard's bed holding his brother in his arms. Twice during the night, Richard had bad coughing spells, but there wasn't any bloody mucus.

The next day, his brother ate a decent breakfast while Abner savored every bite of his. Richard teased him about all the food he ate, his sister teased him about getting fat.

During the day, Abner helped his father cut and bring in more firewood. He played chess with his brother until Richard fell asleep on the sofa. Abner caught his family up on the recent news, and what was going on with his friends.

While the family slept that night, Richard woke up in a terrible coughing fit. This time, there was a lot of bloody mucus. The family rushed into the room. He couldn't breathe lying down, so Abner sat up and held him. The boy was burning up with fever as his mother wiped his face with a cool cloth.

Richard gasped for breath as blood trickled down his chin. He shook, choked, his head fell back on Abner's chest, and he went limp in his brother's arms.

His mother shouted, "Richard, look at me! Say

something to me, honey!"

Her husband took Luella in his arms and said, "He's gone to heaven. He's not suffering anymore."

Eva wrapped her arms around Abner and Richard and pleaded, "Please wake up, Richard! Don't leave us! Come back!"

Abner wept as he held his brother and sister in his arms. Richard was too young to die. His family was going to be devastated, because Richard was such a happy, lovable child. Abner looked at his brother's angelic face and kissed him tenderly goodbye.

He thought, "Lord, take Richard into your loving arms and give him his angel wings, so he can fly through the heavens."

A few days later at Moss Neck, the friends were wondering where Abner might be. He was two days late, and everybody was worried he might be a deserter, but Abner wasn't that kind of person. It just didn't make any sense.

Finally, they saw him walking into camp, so they rushed over to greet him. Their reunion was sweet until the lieutenant stomped over to them.

He yelled, "You're two days late, Pvt Moss!"

The devil flew into Abner and he shouted, "I buried my eight year old brother, so if you want to court martial me for that then go right ahead! I don't care! Take that pistol in your holster and shoot me dead, right now, because I don't care!"

David pulled the lieutenant aside and warned, "Sir, you need to let this go. If you don't, Company I will go all the way to Gen Lee if we have to!"

The lieutenant replied, "I'm so sorry for your loss, Pvt Moss. I didn't know. I'm not a heartless beast."

Some of the men were able to spend Christmas at home while others could go over New Years. The men were finally paid for eight month's service. The troops busied themselves with cutting firewood, running trap lines, and hunting. However, food was still scarce even with family goodies ferried into camp.

To help with morale, Gen Hill had camp musicians put on shows for the men. The troops enjoyed dancing even though it was with each other. Square dancing was the all-time favorite. When it snowed, snowball fights were quite popular.

At times, Gen Hill had to send out provost guard parties to round up all the shirkers that slipped away to go home. Most of the time, the punishment wasn't severe. The worst cases either were sentenced to hard labor or a spell at Castle Prison in Richmond.

During winter quarters, Pvt William Bloxton died from variola. In April, the company lost two men to desertion. In May, they lost one man to desertion.

During this period, Gen Lee sent part of his army south along the James River to collect supplies, food, and forage for the animals.

All the men knew when spring came around the fighting would start again. Most thought the Union army would try to cross the Rappahannock River for the second time in force and push towards Richmond. Would they burn Fredericksburg to the ground? Would they loot and kill innocent civilians? Every man in the 47th Virginia knew they had to stop the Union army, somehow. Every man pondered whether the war would end in 1863. Would they live through this year of conflict?

CHAPTER 6

In February at Moss Neck, several men were cutting firewood and spreading rumors like most soldiers did.

Pvt Brenton stated, "I heard President Lincoln got rid of Gen Burnside."

David asked, "Who did he appoint commander of the Army of the Potomac?"

Pvt Curtis answered, "Somebody named Joseph Hooker is the new general."

Aaron remarked, "We were having such a good time whipping up on Gen Burnside."

Pvt Ball laughed and replied, "I guess that means we git to whip on this here Gen Hooker."

Pvt Brewer commented, "I hope Clay and Gus bring us some fresh meat for supper."

David continued, "Let's hope Micah and Abner have some furry friends caught in their trap lines."

Pvt Patterson laughed and said, "I was on picket duty the other night when I almost shot a darn raccoon. He scared the bejesus out of me."

Pvt Payne added, "At least, it wasn't a skunk. If a skunk sprays you, the whole camp will make you build a hut two miles from here."

Pvt Curtis mentioned, "You know what don't make no sense? We can go several days without fresh meat, and then, we'll have lots to eat."

David commented, "I don't understand it either."

Aaron shouted, "Hey, look over there! It looks like the boys have a surprise for us."

Pvt Brewer chimed in, "Sure enough! It looks like three turkeys, a deer, and lots of little furry friends."

Pvt Brenton suggested, "Let's finish cutting this

wood, so we can start preparing for dinner."

Pvt Curtis shouted, "We're going to be eating mighty good tonight!"

In late April, Union Gen Joseph Hooker put his plan in motion to defeat Gen Lee's army. First, the Union cavalry commanded by Gen George Stoneman would cross the Rappahannock River and raid Confederate supply depots along the railroad running between Richmond and Fredericksburg.

Gen Joseph Hooker   Gen George Stoneman

Second, the Union V, XI, and XII Corps would march to Kelly's Ford and cross the Rappahannock River. Then, they would march to Germanna and Ely's Fords and cross the Rapidan River. They would gather at Chancellorsville where the Orange Turnpike and the Orange Plank Road met. Hooker would attack Lee's army from the west.

Third, the Union I Corps, part of the II Corps, and the VI Corps under the command of Gen John Sedgwick would cross the Rappahannock River south of Fredericksburg and attack Gen Jackson's army and the other Confederate units in Fredericksburg such as Gen Lafayette McLaws' division on Marye's Heights.

Gen John Sedgwick   Gen Lafayette McLaws

Between April 27th and April 28th, the Union V, XI, XII, and part of the II Corps crossed the two rivers and gathered around Chancellorsville. Gen Joseph Hooker got to Chancellorsville late on April 30th and made the Chancellor Mansion his headquarters.

Gen Stoneman's cavalry crossed the Rappahannock River on April 30th to start raiding in the Confederate rear.

Gen Sedgwick's troops crossed the Rappahannock River on pontoon bridges south of Fredericksburg on April 29th.

Things were going so well that Gen Hooker had Gen Daniel Sickles move his III Corps out of Falmouth and cross the Rappahannock River during the night of April 30th and May 1st. This gave Hooker about 70,000 troops around Chancellorsville.

When Gen Hooker's intentions became clearer to
Gen Lee, he decided to pull Gen Jackson's Corps away
from Fredericksburg to join Gen Richard Anderson's
division between the Zoan and Tabernacle churches.
Also, Gen Lee ordered Gen Lafayette McLaws' division
to join Gen Anderson's forces.

Gen William Barksdale's brigade was left on Marye's
Heights, and Gen Jubal Early's division was left on
Prospect Hill. Gen John Sedgwick's 40,000 men would
be facing about 11,000 Confederate forces and around
50 cannons.

Before dawn, Gen Stonewall Jackson marched his
men westward. By 8:00 am, Gen Jackson and
Gen Anderson met at Zoan Church. Jackson ordered an
attack for 11:00 am along the Plank Road and Orange
Turnpike.

Gen Hooker ordered his Union Corps to attack eastward
on the River Road, Plank Road, and the Orange
Turnpike. The Battle of Chancellorsville started around
11:30 am on May 1st when the two armies collided.

Civil War canteen

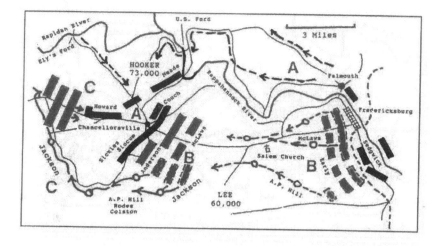

BATTLE - CHANCELLORSVILLE, VIRGINIA
MAY 1-4, 1863

By 2:00 pm, Gen Hooker's men had fought well and made some progress, but Gen Hooker ordered his troops to withdraw back into the Wilderness and set up a defensive position around Chancellorsville. He was going to maintain a defensive fight. He wanted Gen Lee to attack his positions, and not repeat the disaster at Fredericksburg in 1862.

The 450 men of the 47th Virginia along with Gen Hill's Light Division pushed westward on Orange Plank Road passing the Zoan and Tabernacle churches. Gen Jackson ordered his troops to halt four miles from Chancellorsville. The men were ordered to sleep in the field with their weapons.

That evening Gen Lee and Gen Jackson met to discuss the next day's plan of attack. Gen Stuart's cavalry discovered the Union XI Corps was unprotected on the right flank (side). Gen Lee gambled and ordered Gen Jackson's Second Corps to move through the Wilderness on an unfinished railroad cut, and hit the enemy's flank or rear near the Wilderness Church.

Gen Lee & Gen Jackson discuss their plan of attack

Gen Jackson started his corps moving on May 2nd at 4:30 am.

Gus asked, "Where are we going?"

Clay shot back, "How should I know? I guess we're headed towards the enemy."

Abner complained, "Why do we end up in the rear eating everybody else's dust?"

Aaron added, "We've been waiting around forever. It's almost 11:00 am."

By 11:00 am, Gen Hill's Light Division took their position at the end of the column. Gen Jackson's men would have to march 12 miles unseen in order to hit the

Union right.

David commented, "Hey, we're in the Wilderness! Amos lives on the edge of this mess of scrubby trees, thickets, and vines."

Aaron responded, "I didn't know there was a railroad cut in here."

Micah added, "I'm glad this is like a road. We won't get tangled up in all these thickets."

Pvt Curtis remarked, "Maybe, the Yanks won't see us coming."

Late in the afternoon, Gen Jackson formed his men in two battle ranks almost a mile long across the Orange Turnpike. Since Gen Hill's Division was the rear guard, they formed up behind the two battle ranks in reserve.

Gen Jackson ordered his two battle ranks to attack at 5:15 pm. An ocean of screaming gray soldiers erupted out of the woods catching the Union XI Corps cooking dinner with weapons stacked. Union soldiers ran ahead of the Confederate onslaught while Gen Oliver Howard desperately shouted and waved a flag trying to rally his men. Only small groups of men tried to resist before the XI Corps was in total chaotic rout.

Several thousand soldiers took refuge on a hill near the Chancellor Mansion where Union artillery stopped the Confederate advance.

After 7:00 pm, Gen Hill's Light Division was ordered into battle. They pushed up Orange Plank Road and passed the destroyed Van Wert House. They were hit by musket and artillery fire. The 55th Virginia suffered heavy casualties before the division was ordered to camp for the night near an abandoned school.

Gen Jackson leads his troops

That evening, the Confederate army suffered a staggering loss when Gen Jackson was accidently shot by his own men in the woods. He would die from pneumonia on May 10th. Also, that evening, Gen A. P. Hill was wounded under similar circumstances.

The Mortal Wounding of Gen Stonewall Jackson

Gen Jeb Stuart took command of Jackson's Corps, and Gen Henry Heth was given command of the Light Division.

The Union XI Corps suffered 2,500 casualties during the Confederate onslaught.

Gen Henry Heth   Gen Jeb Stuart

On the morning of May 3rd, the Light Division began moving at 5:30 am.

David stood in battle ranks licking his dry lips and thinking about the screams of the wounded caught in the fires burning in the Wilderness. He would rather shoot himself in the head than burn to death.

Clay thinks, "We've had it easy, so far. Two days we've been in the rear guard. Not today! Right up front!"

Aaron asks, "Whose division is behind us?"

Sgt Embrey answers, "Gen Raleigh Colston with Gen Robert Rodes in the rear."

Gus sees Gen Pender's brigade move down the Orange Turnpike to attack Union earthworks and a hill with almost 30 guns on it.

Union artillery

Gen Robert Rodes   Gen Dorsey Pender

Micah sees Gen Lane's brigade move down the south

side of the Orange Turnpike to hit the same earthworks full of Gen Daniel Sickles' III Corps.

Gen Sickles was still furious that Gen Hooker ordered him off Hazel Grove, because it was an excellent artillery platform. Now, the Confederate artillery had batteries on the hill and were pouring shell after shell on his position.

Pender's and Lane's brigades charged the Union fortifications, but were beaten back. Col Brockenbrough ordered his brigade to halt. The 47th and 40th Virginia halted on the south side of the turnpike.

Abner yelled, "Sweet Jesus, the 55th and 22nd haven't stopped! They're charging the earthworks!"

David shouted, "They don't have any support! They're being cut to pieces!"

Col Brockenbrough ordered the 40th and 47th Virginia

to charge the Union position called Fairview. Both
regiments came under heavy fire as they poured volley
after volley into the Union ranks.

David stepped over wounded and dead soldiers from
his brother regiments and fired at will.

Aaron thinks, "My God, the ground is shaking! There
are so many wounded!"

Micah takes ammunition from a dead comrade, loads,
and fires.

Clay's musket is shot out of his hands and rendered
useless. He grabs another musket from a dead comrade.

Gus yells, "You alright, Clay?"

Clay smiles just as a shell explodes near them. The
brothers hit the ground hard. Gus sees stars and
realizes his nose is bleeding and probably broken. He
spits dirt from his mouth and wipes blood running from
his nose. He gets up, grabs his musket, and fires.

Clay gets up, loads the musket, and takes aim at a
Union soldier, and fires.

Clay thinks, "Sweet Jesus, I shot him in the face!"

Abner sees Pvt James Cox wounded in the right arm and Pvt Charles Jones in the left arm.

David sees Pvt Lewis Madison wounded in the gut. He knows Lewis will most likely die. Being gut shot was the wound all soldiers feared the most.

Micah sees Color Sgt Charles Schooler wounded in the right arm and leg. He struggled to keep the regimental flag waving.

Micah grabs Color Sgt Schooler to hold him up.

Color Sgt Schooler yells, "I will not drop the flag!"

Micah shouts, "Charlie, you're badly wounded. You need to go to the rear!"

"I will not leave our flag!"

Micah shouts, "I'll help you! You are a darn fool!"

As the two regiments neared the fortifications many Union soldiers fled towards the hill called Fairview.

Aaron reaches the trenches and comes bayonet to bayonet with a young Union soldier. They plow into each other, wrestle, and Aaron pulls out his knife. He buries the knife into the soldier's neck. The young soldier goes limp.

He thinks, "Please Lord, forgive me for killing this kid. It was him or me."

The regiments take the trenches and chase the retreating troops towards Fairview. Without support, the regiments are recalled by Col Brockenbrough.

Abner helps Micah take Color Sgt Schooler to the rear for medical help.

David, Clay, and Gus help bring back wounded from the battlefield. David finds Aaron and is relieved his brother only has a broken nose.

David remarked, "You look awful! You have two

black eyes and a crooked nose."

Aaron fires back, "Well smart mouth, your face and teeth are black."

David teased, "I can wash my black gunpowder off my face."

"I'm hurting here. Give me some sympathy."

Later on during the day, Col Brockenbrough ordered the 40th and 47th Virginia to re-take Fairview which they held for the rest of the day.

Gen Hooker ordered his troops to dig in north of the Orange Plank Road and hold their ground on May 4th and May 5th.

During the early morning of May 5th, Gen John Sedgwick retreated across the river. When Gen Hooker was told this, he felt his campaign was doomed. On the night of May 5th and May 6th, Hooker and his artillery crossed the river first. On May 6th at 6:00 am, the infantry followed worrying the rains might cause the pontoon bridges to give way.

Gen Lee was upset that he couldn't launch one final attack to crush the Union army at Chancellorsville. Gen Hooker and his army had slipped away.

Of the 60,000 men in Gen Lee's army that were involved in the fighting, 13,300 were casualties. The Union army suffered around 17,200 casualties out of 133,000 troops engaged.

The Light Division left for Camp Gregg on May 7th. Gen Lee re-organized his corps after the death of Gen Stonewall Jackson. The 47th Virginia was placed in Gen A. P. Hill's III Corps, Gen Henry Heth's division, and

Col Brockenbrough's brigade.

Again, Judge Arthur Murphy kept his family together and safe during the Battle of Chancellorsville. News spread like wildfire that Gen Lee had soundly defeated the Army of the Potomac. However, the family was very upset when they learned Gen Jackson had been killed. The boys had always spoken highly of their corps commander. Who would replace him?

Gen Lee decided to take the summer campaigning to the North. He wasn't about to let the Union dictate upcoming battles. Virginia was war-ravaged and needed a break from marching armies. He would invade Maryland and Pennsylvania collecting badly needed supplies and food. In other words, take the war to them.

Around June 3, 1863, Gen James Longstreet's I Corps and Gen Richard Ewell's II Corps headed northwest towards the Blue Ridge Mountains. The I and II Corps camped near Culpeper by June 5th. Gen Lee ordered Gen Stuart to cross the Rappahannock River and raid Union supply depots and camps, so the Union wouldn't know about Confederate movements.

Colt Army Pistol

Gen James Longstreet   Gen Richard Ewell

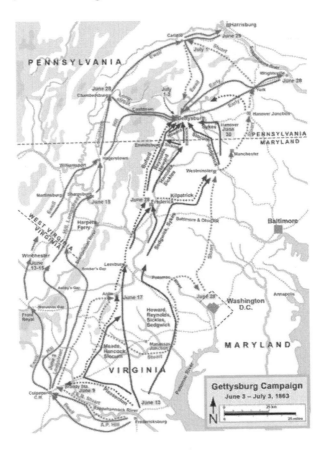

Gen A. P. Hill was left in Fredericksburg to make the Union forces think Lee's entire army was still there.

By June 12th, Gen Ewell's II Corps crossed the Blue Ridge Mountains at Chester Gap.

On June 14th, Gen A. P. Hill left Fredericksburg when Gen Hooker withdrew northward to stay between Washington, D. C. and Gen Lee.

By June 15th, Gen Ewell's II Corps started crossing the Potomac River close to Hagerstown, Maryland.

Gen Hill's III Corps and Gen Longstreet's I Corps crossed the Potomac on June 24th and June 25th.

President Lincoln wasn't pleased with Gen Joseph Hooker's performance at Chancellorsville nor his slow pursuit of Gen Lee's army. On June 27th, the President replaced Gen Hooker with Gen George Meade.

On June 14th, Col Brockenbrough's brigade left Fredericksburg to catch up with Gen Hill's Corps, because they were the rear guard. They marched about 12 miles a day in the June heat. The 47th Virginia marched through Front Royal, Berryville, and then crossed the Potomac River on June 26th.

During the next three days, Gen Hill's Corps marched through Chambersburg, Fayetteville, and reached Cashtown, Pennsylvania on June 29th. They were only eight miles from Gettysburg.

By June 29th, Gen Lee's army was in an arc from Chambersburg to Carlisle to near Harrisburg, Pennsylvania. Gen Lee wanted to gather his troops around Cashtown before he engaged the enemy. He ordered his generals not to attack the enemy until all his forces were together. As fate would have it, that didn't happen.

Gen Henry Heth sent Gen Johnston Pettigrew's brigade to Gettysburg to look for supplies on June 30th. Gen Pettigrew returned to Cashtown after noticing Union cavalry south of the town.

Gen A. P. Hill made the decision to perform a reconnaissance to find out how many Union troops were in Gettysburg. Where was the Confederate cavalry commanded by Gen Stuart? They were supposed to be the eyes of the army.

On the morning of July 1st, Gen Heth marched towards Gettysburg with Maj William Pegram's artillery, Gen James Archer's brigade, and Gen Joseph Davis' brigade in the July heat on Chambersburg Pike.

Union Gen John Buford knew he had to utilize three ridges west of town to stop, or, at least, delay Confederate forces until the Union infantry could get there. He only had a little over 2,700 troopers, but some of them had breech-loading carbines. This meant, they could fire two to three times faster, and the troopers didn't have to stand to reload. Every trooper knew they had to stop the Confederates, because this was Union soil for heaven's sake!

Maj William Pegram

Gen John Buford

The 47th Virginia and Col Brockenbrough's brigade waited their turn to march from Cashtown.

Abner complained, "Here we go, again! Why do we end up at the rear of the division?"

Micah complained, "We'll be eating everybody else's dust. I guess we're Gen Heth's stepchild."

Gus fired back, "We must be the general's orphan child."

Abner asked, "I ain't heard of no town called Gettysburg. Why are we going there?"

Cpl Watson answered, "Maybe, we can get lots of supplies from the fine folks of the town."

Clay chimed in, "Maybe, we can take a bath when we get there."

Gus complained, "It's darn hot! My shoes are full of sweat!"

David remarked, "There will be lots of fellers running to the bushes with dia-ree."

Aaron agreed, "Ya, between cherries and the heat,

they're running us to death."

Abner complained, "All of us smell like an outhouse."

Gus shot back, "I wouldn't know, because my nose is dead."

Pvt Brewer agreed, "My nose can't even smell a skunk camped out on my head."

Pvt Lowry commented, "At least, we have more to eat thanks to Maryland and Pennsylvania."

Pvt Lewis Payne mentioned, "I was plum disappointed to find out Pennsylvania has bloodsucking mosquitoes, too."

Pvt Skidmore shot back, "They ain't as big as Virginia mosquitoes."

David whispered in his brother's ear, "I got a bad feeling about this. If the Yankee Gen Meade's army gets here time enough, we're in for a big fight. I don't think Meade moves like a snail like Hooker."

Aaron agreed, "I'm thinking the same thing."

Pvt Thomas West responded, "Well, Gen Lee will whip up on the Yankees just like he did at Chancellorsville."

Aaron stated, "It's going to be a knockdown, knuckle-busting fight, for sure boys!"

Abner shot back, "I'm ready for a street fighting brawl after what they did to Fredericksburg."

Sgt J. P. Jones suggested, "Just keep thinking about Fredericksburg. Remember,
Gen Lee will not tolerate looting from us."

Lt Stewart shouted, "Alright men, form up and start marching."

Pvt Langley complained, "I hate marching and fighting in the summer when it's hot as hades."

Cpl Watson responded, "The next time I see Gen Lee I'll make sure to tell him."

The men of the 47th Virginia laughed, fell into line, and marched towards their destiny at a small crossroads town called Gettysburg. Some would not survive July 1st, and others would add their blood on this soon to be hallowed ground. Each man entered his private world of thoughts to prepare himself for battle.

By 7:30 am, Gen Heth's two brigades ran into cavalry skirmishers about three miles west of town. The brigades formed a line across Chambersburg Pike and ran into dismounted cavalry hiding behind fence posts using rapid fire breech-loading carbines. The Union troopers delayed the Confederates as long as they could around Herr's Ridge.

By 10:30 am, the Confederates pushed the Union cavalry back to McPherson's Ridge. All of a sudden, the Union I Corps commanded by Gen John Reynolds arrived and took up positions on either side of Chambersburg Pike.

Confederate Gen Joseph Davis' brigade ran into Union Gen Lysander Cutler's brigade near Willoughby Run and an unfinished railroad bed. The fighting was so furious that Cutler's brigade lost almost half its men as casualties in less than 30 minutes. The 147th New York Infantry lost over half its men as casualties.

Ammunition

Gen John Reynolds   Gen Lysander Cutler

On the other side of Chambersburg Pike, Gen Archer's Alabama and Tennessee boys ran into Union Gen Solomon Meredith's Iron Brigade troops from Michigan, Wisconsin, and Indiana.

Gen John Reynolds was killed while ordering his men to attack near Herbst Woods. Gen Archer became the first general captured in Gen Lee's army. Pvt Patrick Moloney from the 6th Wisconsin was awarded the Medal of Honor for capturing the general.

Death of Gen Reynolds

Gen Heth's last two brigades and Gen Dorsey Pender's division reached the battlefield around 12:30 pm.

Pettigrew's North Carolina boys, and Brockenbrough's Virginia boys formed up in a battle line along Herr's Ridge with the 47th Virginia on the far left flank by the Chambersburg Pike. Around 2:30 pm, the battle line stormed towards McPherson's Ridge.

Cpl Watson reminded, "Make every shot count!"

Lt Stewart yells, "Forward men!"

David sucked in a deep breath. The air was so hot and humid. It was so hard to breathe. His hair was wet and sticky. The air reeked with the smell of gunpowder and death. He still had a bad feeling about this place.

Gen Pettigrew's brigade attacked and pushed the Iron Brigade towards the Lutheran Theological Seminary. The 26th North Carolina made up of 839 men suffered around 525 casualties. The 24th Michigan casualties were around 399 men out of 496. Gen Henry Heth was shot in the head and remained unconscious for over 24 hours.

The 47th Virginia crossed Willoughby Run as fresh Union troops entered the battle. Company I was marching between Company H and K.

The musket fire, exploding shells, and the screams of the wounded roared in Aaron's head. Suddenly, Pvt William West dropped, wounded in the left arm.

Aaron yelled, "West is badly wounded, David!"

"We have to keep moving!"

Suddenly, David is sprayed with blood and trips over a body. He crawls to the man and discovers it's Lt William Stewart.

"Oh God, Lieutenant! Why did you have to die?"

The companies get mixed together trying to keep their battle line.

Clay fires off a shot when Cpl John Watson screams in agony.

Clay yells, "Stay down Cpl Watson! You're hit in the thigh. I'll come back for you."

The regiment is ordered to fall back and re-group. Clay helps Watson to his feet and helps him get to the surgeons.

As Micah falls back, he stumbles upon Lt Addison Crittenden from Company F wounded in the stomach. Micah picks him up and takes him to the rear.

Abner stumbles upon Pvt Henry Isabell from Company K wounded in the leg. He helps him fall back to safety.

Gus sees Pvt James Lee and Sgt Robert Moore from Company B lying dead on the battlefield.

Col Brockenbrough's brigade re-groups and launches a second attack.

Gettysburg July 1

David felt like they were fighting in a large bowl. There were battles raging in every direction. He was stepping over the dead and wounded trying to see through the smoke that hung like a curtain, at times.

The line fires a volley, and David reloads, as quickly as possible. A bullet hisses by his head.

"Oh God, that was close!"

Micah wipes sweat out of his eyes, takes aim, and fires. A shell explodes nearby spraying the men with grass, dirt, and shrapnel. Pvt Thomas West drops next to Micah.

West yells, "Help me! I can't feel my hand!"

Micah leans down and promises, "I'll try to come back for you!"

Brockenbrough's men desperately tried to break through the Union lines, but are ordered to fall back and re-group. By 3:00 pm, the 47th Virginia's brigade re-groups and attacks for the third time. Finally, they break the Union line, and some of the Union troops retreat through the narrow streets of Gettysburg towards Cemetery Hill. The brigade is exhausted and is low or out of ammunition. The men drop like flies from the oppressive heat and fatigue unable to chase the enemy any further.

David panted and tried to suck in as much air as he could. He didn't have the energy to sit up, let alone stand. He drank his canteen dry and emptied another one off a dead Yankee. Every muscle in his body shook and cramped.

Aaron fell to his knees and gagged. He was burning up, so he took his jacket off and poured water all over his head and face.

Clay dropped to his knees as his world spun around. Suddenly, his world turned black as he passed out.

Micah collapsed with only enough energy to empty his canteen. Gus unbuttoned Micah's jacket and poured water over him. Gus got his jacket off, drank water, and dropped to the ground in an exhaustive sleep.

Abner dropped to his knees and watched sweat drop from his hair and face onto the ground. His heart was pounding in his chest and ears as he slumped to the ground unable to move.

Gen Dorsey Pender's division marched through Gen Heth's exhausted and battered men around 4:00 pm. One of the brigades that stepped through Col Brockenbrough's men was commanded by Gen Alfred Scales. He had five regiments of North Carolinians totaling 1,400 men. They charged an area supported by 20 Union guns that fired shells, canister, and double canister shots into the brigade. There would be only 500 men left standing commanded by one lieutenant.

Gen Alfred Scales

On the Union side, the 16th Maine made up of 298 men was ordered to hold its position, so the rest of the brigade could escape. When the holding action was over, there was only 35 survivors left.

The Union I and XI Corps commanded by Gen Oliver Howard stopped the Confederate onslaught at Cemetery Hill and prayed for reinforcements. Gen George Meade sent his trusted II Corps commander Gen Winfield Hancock to take command of the Union troops until he could get there from Taneytown, Maryland.

Gen George Meade   Gen Winfield Hancock

When the II and III Corps arrived, Gen Hancock placed them on Cemetery Ridge. Now, the Union had the high ground. Gen Lee would have to defeat the Union troops on their high ground if he wanted to win the battle.

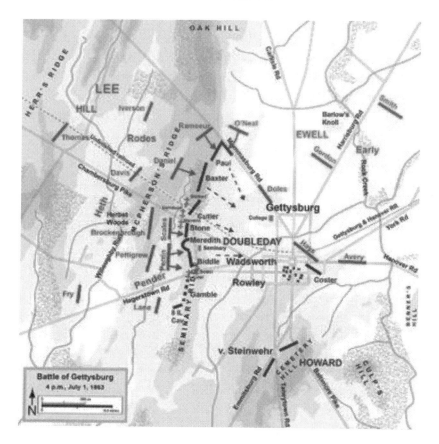

Finally, the 47th Virginia and the rest of the brigade were able to get up and move back towards Seminary Ridge. The men helped the wounded get to the hospital tents, if they could. The dead would have to wait.

David looked around the hospital tents in disbelief. There were so many wounded suffering in agony. Lt Henry Garrett from Company E was shot in the knee, Pvt Richard Peed from Company C was shot in the thigh, and Pvt Robert Warwick from Company F was lying dead on the ground.

Aaron walked over to David and said in a trembling voice, "The surgeon had to amputate Henry Isabell's leg."

Clay came over and said, "I hope he makes it, poor devil. Come on ya'll. Let's get some food and try to get some sleep."

Amid all this horror, one still needed to eat and sleep.

None of the friends could think about eating, but they knew they needed as much as they could get down.

Gus ate as much as he could hold and thought about how peaceful the sky looked. All around the cries of the wounded could be heard under that peaceful sky. He drifted off to sleep, because he was so weary.

Micah thought about Grace and wondered if he would survive this battle. Thinking about her helped him keep his sanity.

Abner ate and wondered, "Have I died and gone to hades? I'm surrounded by a mass of suffering humanity and tormented souls. How can any of us survive this gruesome horror?"

The troops in reserve on this horrible day brought back ammunition, muskets, and anything else useful that was left on the battlefield. Some muskets had several rounds jammed in the barrel which the owner failed to fire.

More Confederate troops arrived during the evening and the next morning not knowing what carnage awaited them.

On July 1st, the Union had 22,000 men involved in the fighting. They suffered close to 9,000 casualties.

The Confederate troops involved in the first day numbered 27,000 men. They suffered a little over 6,000 casualties.

On July 2nd, Gen Lee held Gen Heth's division in

reserve and decided to attack the Union left focusing on Little Round Top.

On July 3rd, Gen Lee chose troops commanded by Gen George Pickett, Gen Johnston Pettigrew, and Gen Isaac Trimble to attack the Union center along Cemetery Ridge.

Gen Lee believed 12,500 men could breech the weak Union center after a massive cannonade from the Confederate artillery. The artillery would destroy its Union counterpart, so the men could march about three-quarters of a mile over open fields, scale fences, and capture the high ground.

Gen Pickett's division and Col Brockenbrough's brigade were Virginians. The other troops were from North Carolina, Alabama, Tennessee, and Mississippi.

Gen A. P. Hill was ill, so the men chosen for the July 3rd attack were ones who had been in the heavy fighting on July 1st. Most of the rest of Hill's Corps had fought a little or not at all during July 1st and July 2nd. Fresh troops should have been chosen for the July 3rd attack.

Gen George Pickett   Gen Isaac Trimble

Gen Edward Johnson

Gen Lee wanted to attack Culp's Hill on the Union right with Gen Edward Johnson's boys while Gen Pickett attacked the Union center. As fate would have it, the attack on Culp's Hill raged for seven hours and ended when the Confederate artillery started its cannonade against the Union center. Gen Lee didn't capture Culp's Hill.

By 1:00 pm, about 160 guns started firing on Union positions along a two mile front. A lot of Confederate shells didn't detonate, because of poor fuses. Many shells overshot their mark and landed behind the infantry.

Union artillery chief, Gen Henry Hunt, ordered his 80 guns to slowly cease firing to make the Rebels think they were destroying the Union guns. Gen Hunt knew he needed to save ammunition, so he could support his infantry.

Between 2:00 pm and 3:00 pm, the Confederate regiments stepped out of the Seminary Ridge woods in a mile long line. The day was hot and humid with a temperature of 87 degrees.

Col Brockenbrough's brigade was on the far left of the Confederate line facing Ziegler's Grove. The 47th and 55th Virginia were the end of the line. There were no troops behind them for support. Little did they know that 1,600 shells would be fired at them from Cemetery Hill. They would be walking into a smoke filled valley of death.

The order to move forward was given, and the 47th Virginia marched into madness. The Union cannons opened fire as the regiment marched towards the Bliss barn. The regiment marched passed the barn as artillery shells rained down on them. The companies got mixed together trying to dress the line.

Aaron yells, "We can't dress the line, because the shells are blowing holes in our ranks faster than we can close them!"

Gus is covered in blood, flesh, hair, and yells, "Sweet Jesus, Pvt Joseph Wrentone is dead! Oh God, help me! His blood is all over me!"

David sees Pvt John White from Company C fall, shot in the chest. He looks to his left just as Lt John Rollins from Company E falls. David leans over and sees there is no hope for John.

Clay feels someone grab his leg. He bends down to see Pvt Francis White from Company C badly wounded in the leg. Clay's musket is ripped from his hands by a piece of shrapnel. He takes another musket from Pvt William Burruss from Company H who is badly wounded in the right hip and arm. He pushes on through the dead and wounded.

When the 47th and the 55th Virginia are within rifle range, the 8th Ohio Infantry crashes into them from the flank. Pvt Thomas West from Company I is hit in the arm and falls. The two Virginia regiments take cover in a sunken road.

Micah yells, "We don't have any support!"

Exploding shells rain debris down on the men.

Abner yells, "Sweet Jesus, the Yanks are charging us from two sides!"

Each man knows they don't have a chance if they stay in the sunken road. The artillery will zero in on them, and the 8th Ohio will overrun them.

David asks, "Where is Col Mayo?"

Aaron answers, "I ain't seen him."

Micah asks, "Where is Col Brockenbrough?"

Abner yells back, "I ain't seen him, neither!"

David looks at the sergeant and yells, "If we stay here, we're going to die or get captured! My God Sergeant, we don't have any support!"

From somewhere, the men hear the order to fall back. The order races through the ranks, and the men fall back by Stevens Run, the Bliss barn, and head towards Seminary Ridge. The men pick up as many wounded as they can, but some will be captured.

Clay panted, wiped sweat, and asked, "Why didn't we have support, Sergeant?"

He answered, "I don't know. I don't mind fighting, but don't throw me to the wolves to be slaughtered."

Gus shouts, "My God, look at Gen Pickett's boys! The Yanks are pouring canister shot at them. Our men are dropping in scores!"

The men watch in horror as the gray wave continues to get smaller and smaller. The gray wave rolls over the small stone fence in one area, but starts to recede. The blue line holds, and the once magnificent gray ribbons flowing across that mile wide slope recede in bits and shredded pieces. Most of the proud flags waving in the breeze are gone along with their color bearers.

Pickett's Charge

Fifty per cent casualties would be suffered among most of the nine Confederate brigades that took part in Pickett's Charge. Union casualties suffered were around 1,500 men. Confederate casualties suffered were over 6,500 men. Eleven regimental commanders from Gen Pickett's division were wounded or killed.

As the wounded struggled to get back to Seminary Ridge after an hour of madness, the Confederates prepared for a counterattack from the Yankees. The attack didn't happen, because both sides were exhausted.

The Stone Wall on Cemetery Ridge

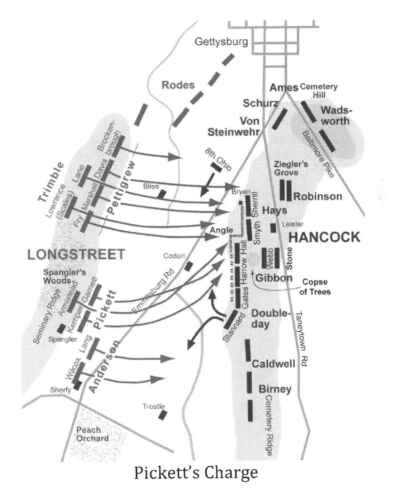

Pickett's Charge

On July 4th, both sides tended to their wounded and some dead. Along Chambersburg Pike wagons gathered from Gen Heth's division to transport the wounded back to Virginia. About 700 wounded and sick would have to be left behind. From the 47th Virginia, Dr. William Spence, Jr. would stay behind to take care of those that were too serious to move.

The 47ᵗʰ Virginia lost the following men killed or mortally wounded at Gettysburg. Company I was down to 22 men.

Pvt James Anderson	Lt Addison Crittenden
Pvt William Brewer	Lt William Stewart
Pvt Robert Warwick	Pvt Thomas West
Sgt Robert Moore	Pvt James Lee
Pvt William Pomeroy	Lt John Rollins
Pvt Joseph Wrentone	Pvt Francis White

During the night of July 4ᵗʰ, Gen Heth's division started down the Fairfield Road during a heavy rainstorm.

David commented, "Heaven is trying to wash the blood from this place."

Aaron added, "Heaven is trying to wash my soul clean."

Micah remarked, "I will never feel clean, even when the war is over."

Gus predicted, "I don't think we'll ever invade the

North, again."

Clay suggested, "The Yankees ain't running like they used to. Maybe, this here
Gen Meade is better at fighting."

Pvt Curtis complained, "I hate marching in the pouring rain and stomping through mud."

Pvt W. Patterson agreed, "I do, too. The poor wounded are really suffering in the wagons."

Abner commented, "The sooner we git to Virginia the better I'll like it."

By July 7th, the 47th Virginia reached Hagerstown, Maryland. Gen Lee was informed that many of his soldiers were ransacking the town looking for food and supplies. Lee ordered some of his regiments, including the 47th Virginia, to serve as provost guards to stop the looting. However, it was too late to stop many soldiers from getting crazy drunk. Among those drunken soldiers was Col Mayo from the 47th Virginia. Of course, he was arrested and later court martialed.

By July 10th, the Confederate army entrenched around Williamsport and Falling Waters hoping the flooded Potomac River would drop quickly, so they could cross back into Virginia. The Union cavalry was constantly attacking the retreating army, and now the Union infantry was bearing down on them.

By early July 14th, Gen Heth's division was the rearguard of the army. The three brigades set up positions on high ground with a clearing and then woods in front of them. The worn out men of the rearguard slept on the ground while the wagons and artillery slowly crossed the Potomac River on pontoon bridges.

Capt Brooke called the friends together and ordered, "Since the six of you are crack shots, I want you down by the river and pontoon bridge in case Yankee cavalry comes charging out of nowhere."

David asked, "Are there sharpshooters on the other side of the river?"

"Yes. Now, spread out, but keep each other in sight."

The friends saluted, grabbed their gear, and headed for the river.

Abner complained, "I'm so tired I'm not sure if I can keep my eyes open and alert."

Micah shot back, "If you fall asleep, you might not open your eyes, again."

Gus chimed in, "That's the honest truth, Abner."

Around 11:00 am, the friends started hearing musket fire and braced themselves for an attack. The men were ordered to set up on the Virginia side of the river to cover the last remnants of the Confederate army to cross.

The 6th Michigan Cavalry charged the exhausted Confederates. The first attack was beaten back. Capt Thomas Dew, Lt Peyton Moncure, the color bearers from the 40th, 47th, and 55th Virginia, and Drummer William Rosson led the charge against the retreating cavalry.

When the charge started, Gen A. P. Hill had already ordered his men to withdraw, but the colonel ordered his men to charge around the colors. The brigade commander withdrew and crossed the pontoon bridge while the brigade attacked.

All three regimental flags were captured. First

Sergeant Charles Holton from the 7th Michigan Cavalry, Company C, was awarded the Medal of Honor for capturing the 55th Virginia flag.

The regimental drummer, William Rosson, was captured and later exchanged on February 3, 1864 from Pt. Lookout Prison in Maryland.

The 47th Virginia would have 48 men captured at Falling Waters. Among those was Steptoe Washington, better known as Bigtoe to his friends.

The weary and wounded men kept moving southward to stay ahead of the Union cavalry. They didn't stop until they reached Bunker Hill. Here they would camp for a few days for some badly needed rest.

David looked at his brother and asked, "What's wrong, Aaron? You've been mighty quiet since we crossed the Potomac."

"I can't forget the horrible madness that happened at Gettysburg. I don't know why I'm not dead or wounded. When we got close to the Bliss barn, I saw a color bearer disappear when a shell exploded right in front of him. He was gone; it was as if he never existed. I saw another poor soul lose his arm, because a shell ripped it off. There is no way to describe what a body looks like after double canister shots have riddled it. We walked through the Valley of Madness, and we'll never be whole, again. Part of me is dead inside, David. Plain dead! Dead forever!"

David asked, "Why do you feel dead inside?"

"Because I was glad it wasn't my arm, and my body riddled with canister shots!"

David consoled, "All of us feel the same way. I'm glad I'm not dead or crippled. We can't answer why we're still alive and someone else is dead. I pray every day that I'll be able to hold my wife and son in my arms, again."

Aaron continued, "I'm afraid this war will turn me into a monster that's not fit to love a woman. What kind of monster will I be in Deidre's arms?"

David answered, "I don't know what kind of man each one of us will be if we make it through this war. The only thing we can do is think about all the peaceful, happy times we had and try to block out the horror. Somehow, we've got to stay strong for our families, because they're in danger."

Aaron added, "I pray Poppa takes the family to Uncle Homer's place. You know the Yankees will attack across the Rappahannock River in the spring or before then."

"I pray that, too, because we haven't gotten any mail from our loved ones in months."

Aaron commented, "When we can write letters, I'm not sure they get delivered. Shoot fire! We don't get paid every month, either!"

"Ain't that the honest truth!"

Faces of the Civil War

CHAPTER 7

Judge Murphy heard a knock at the door and grabbed his gun. Everyone knew what they were supposed to do. Abner's father identified himself and Arthur let him inside.

Arthur asked, "How are you doing?"

Mr. Moss answered, "I'm fair, Arthur. I came by to let you know, I'm moving my family to live close to my sister's place."

Arthur asked, "Is that your sister who lives between Bowling Green and Hanover?"

"Yes. I can't make a living here anymore, because so many folks have left to get away from the war. My sister says her area needs a blacksmith and wheelwright real bad. I just don't know what else to do."

Arthur replied, "I have decided to move down with my brother's family in Caroline County. After we heard all the terrible news about Gettysburg, I knew we had to get out. I don't know what has happened to my sons."

"I don't know what has happened to Abner or his friends. So many of our boys were captured at Falling Waters. Are they alive?"

Grace spoke up and said, "Not knowing is driving us crazy. We have no idea where they are."

"I'm glad you're leaving, Arthur. Neither one of us wants the Yankees threatening our women folk and children."

Arthur asked, "When are you leaving?"

"The day after tomorrow."

Mr. Moss asked, "When are you heading out?"

"This weekend. Homer is coming up with a couple of wagons to help us move. We might have to make a couple of trips to move what we need."

Mr. Moss remarked, "I wish you Godspeed and pray for your safety. I'm leaving a note for Abner in case he comes home."

Arthur added, "I'll do the same thing for my boys."

The two men shook hands and said their farewells. No one knew if they would ever see each other, again.

Grace cried and said sadly, "I never thought I'd have to leave our home like this."

Arthur held his daughter and said, "Neither did I, Grace."

Col Brockenbrough's brigade was down to about 300 men while the 47th Virginia had dropped to about 100 men. Losing so many men captured at Falling Waters was a severe blow to all the regiments in the brigade.

Gen Hill replaced Col Brockenbrough on July 19, 1863 with Gen Henry Harrison Walker. The colonel was angry he was replaced and resigned.

By July 25th, the regiment camped near Culpeper Court House. The III Corps reached Orange Court House by August 3rd and stayed there for two months.

Gen Hill went to work making sure his troops got enough rations of meat, potatoes, vegetables, and sugar. Even the wounded and sick were getting much better care than before.

The men built churches, because a religious revival was spreading through the regiments. The men sang hymns and prayed to help heal their tattered souls. It wasn't unusual for a soldier to go to church services several times a week. This helped the men's morale and gave the men a chance to wash some of the blood from their souls.

David noticed that his brother, cousins, and friends enjoyed the revival like so many others. For David and many of the soldiers, it helped heal some of the shattered emotions that had been damaged over so many months of combat.

Things were improving in the 47th Virginia concerning the number of men dying from disease. In 1862, there had been 103 deaths, but in 1863 the number had dropped below twenty.

In 1862, the 47th Virginia had 83 men desert, however, in 1863 the number had dropped below twenty.

Since Col Mayo was in the process of being court martialed, LtCol John Lyell was given command of the regiment.

In September, Union Gen Meade had to send two corps to the Western Theater in Tennessee for the Chattanooga Campaign. Likewise, Gen Lee had to send part of Gen Longstreet's corps to Tennessee as reinforcements for the Battle of Chickamauga. This meant that the two armies in the East were about the same size. Now, Gen Lee had the opportunity to go on the offensive.

In early October, Gen Hill marched his III Corps northward towards Culpeper. Gen Lee's plan was to attack Gen Meade's flank and get between him and Washington, D. C.

By October 13th, the 47th Virginia and Gen Heth's division were near Warrenton. On October 14th, Union and Confederate forces collided at Bristoe Station on the Orange and Alexandria Railroad. Union troops from Gen Hancock's II Corps hid behind a railroad embankment waiting to ambush Confederate forces coming after them. Without knowledge of the area and forces ahead of him, Gen Hill ordered Gen Heth's boys to attack before Gen Heth had all his brigades in battle ranks. Gen Walker's brigade, including the 47th Virginia, had to catch up to the rest of the division.

Sgt Jones ordered, "Double quick, men, we have to catch up."

Gus commented, "How can we run through this thick woods and underbrush? It's almost as bad as the Wilderness."

Sgt Jones fired back, "Move as quickly as you can!"

Clay complained, "I've already tripped twice in this confounded mess!"

Aaron shouted, "I can't see the other brigades, but I can hear a lot of musket fire."

David suggested, "I guess our boys have found the Yankees."

Gen Heth's other two brigades walked into the Union trap and were cut to pieces. By the time Gen Walker's brigade reached the battle, the Confederate troops were retreating. The brigade set up a battle line to cover the withdrawal. Gen Meade's army was able to withdraw to Centreville, safely.

Gen Lee's offensive plans turned into a disaster. The Union army only suffered 540 casualties compared to Gen Lee's 1,380 casualties. Gen Heth's casualties made up over 800 of those. Fortunately, the 47th Virginia was spared any casualties.

Gen Hill's III Corps spent October 15th and 16th destroying miles of track on the Orange and Alexandria Railroad. On October 18th, the Confederate army crossed the Rappahannock River, and the 47th Virginia spent the rest of the month not far from Culpeper.

The Army of the Potomac spent a month replacing the tracks the Confederates had destroyed after the Battle of Bristoe Station.

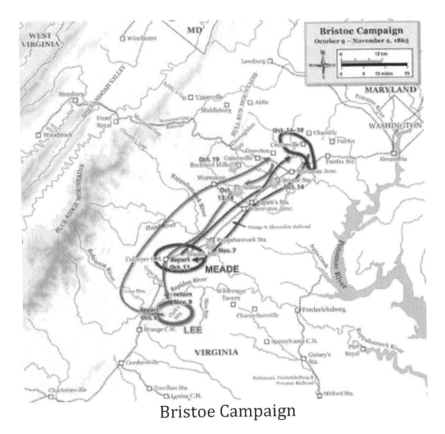

Bristoe Campaign

In early November, Gen Meade's VI Corps attacked the Confederate forces at Rappahannock Station (present-day Remington, Virginia) and captured over

1,600 of Gen Jubal Early's men.

Five miles downstream another Union corps crossed the Rappahannock River at Kelly's Ford.

The 6th Maine swarmed over the Confederate eastern redoubt, and the 5th Wisconsin plowed through the defenders at the western redoubt. Col Emory Upton's troops smashed through their section resulting in the surrender of hundreds of Rebel soldiers. Many Rebel soldiers swam the icy Rappahannock or ran across the pontoon bridge hoping not to be shot before they could reach the other side.

Gen Lee decided to pull back south of the Rapidan River, because he didn't want Gen Meade to pin his army against the Rapidan. Gen Lee couldn't afford to over extend his lines of supply. The Union army was sitting on their supply base and could get whatever they needed, quickly.

Confederate casualties numbered over 1,600 men while the Union only suffered a little over 400 men.

Gen Walker's brigade marched in the snow to cross the Rapidan River. By November 11th, the 47th Virginia was close to Orange Court House.

On November 26th, Gen Meade went on the offensive and crossed the Rapidan River and turned west intending to attack Gen Lee's flank. Gen Heth's division found themselves marching down Orange Plank Road eastward. The two armies skirmished several times trying to overrun the other. The following day Gen Heth's division withdrew behind Mine Run and went about building formidable breastworks.

Gen Meade decided not to attack the Confederate's strong fortifications, so he withdrew around December 1st. The Union general's Mine Run Campaign came to an end.

The 47th Virginia went back to one of their former camps near Orange Court House.

The regiment suffered 12 casualties during the campaign. Nine men were captured when they were cut off from their skirmish line by the Yankees.

Maj James Bruce was wounded in the left shoulder and arm. The surgeon had to amputate his arm to save his life. Lt John Peyton Jones from Company I was wounded in the right arm.

The winter months would be very difficult on Gen Walker's brigade. Not only did they have to chase the Union cavalry, they had to endure Virginia's unpredictable weather.

The brigade went about building shanties with tree branches and mud fireplaces for their winter quarters. The regiment would rather be close to Fredericksburg, but that didn't happen.

In the middle of December, Gen Walker's brigade left their shanties, boarded a train to Staunton, and found out they would be protecting Staunton during the winter months from raiding Yankee cavalry. This time the Yankee cavalry didn't show up near Staunton like rumors had said.

The brigade marched west of Staunton to Buffalo Gap looking for the Yankee cavalry rumored to be there.

David complained, "It just had to start raining and sleeting."

Aaron complained, "I hate marching in the sleet and snow. They ran our behinds out of Orange telling us we'd be back, shortly. Our oilcloths are back in the shanties."

Clay added, "This is when we need our oilcloths and extra blankets."

Micah shot back, "From now on, my oilcloth is coming with me."

Abner complained, "I hate snow and sleet. I'm freezing to death!"

Gus added, "My feet are frozen. They feel like blocks of ice."

Aaron remarked, "I don't think I can load my musket, because my hands are frozen."

On December 17th, the brigade marched back to Staunton, because they didn't find any Yankee cavalry. It turned out to be another wild goose chase.

When the brigade got back to Staunton, many of the men begged the townspeople to give them shelter from the snow. The friends were lucky enough to find two families that took them in.

Between December 19th and January 10, 1864, the brigade chased the Union cavalry from Staunton to Mount Jackson in the snow and freezing temperatures. Several men were fighting bad colds and coughs, praying they wouldn't get pneumonia.

Between January 10th and 29th, the chasing continued from Staunton to Mount Jackson. Finally, the brigade set up winter quarters close to Harrisonburg. The men in the 47th Virginia were paid and received mail during this period.

The Murphy boys were very relieved when they found out their father had moved in with their Uncle Homer. Abner was glad his father got his family out of Fredericksburg.

In early March 1864, the brigade was so happy to be leaving the Shenandoah Valley and going back to their camp near Orange Court House. The closer they could get to home the better. They all felt in the spring the Union army would be crossing the Rappahannock and Rapidan Rivers.

In late March, it was getting quite cold and the gray skies were building.

Homer walked into the farmhouse with Arthur and said, "Lord is it cold! My bones are telling me bad weather is coming soon. When we finish lunch, you boys bring lots of firewood up on the porch and inside."

Teddy replied, "Yes sir, Uncle Homer."

Arthur added, "We'll tend to the barn, cows, and horses."

Homer suggested, "Leann, take Grace with you and take care of the chickens."

"Yes sir, Poppa."

Ellen looked at Deidre and said, "We'll bring more food inside and put it in the root cellar."

Ty asked, "Poppa, do you want me to run my trap lines?"

"Yes, just as soon as you finish with the firewood. If it starts snowing, you git back to the house in a hurry."

Harry asked, "Do you think it will snow, Poppa?"

"I believe so, because the wind is blowing from the northwest. When I finish in the barn, I'll help Ty. Maybe, we'll git a deer."

After eating, everyone went to work preparing for the coming weather. Ellen knew her husband had a knack for changes in the weather. It had been mild, but Virginia was notorious for crazy weather.

The following day was March 22nd, and the two families got busy after breakfast doing their chores. Homer and Ty got a deer and a wild turkey the day before, so they were finishing them up for cooking. It started to snow, and the wind started to howl. Chores were done as quickly as possible, so everyone could get inside and enjoy the warmth from the fireplaces.

Grace was looking out the window and said, "It's snowing real hard, and the snow is blowing all over the place."
Homer asked, "Can you see the barn?"
"I can see it, so far, Uncle Homer."

Not far away, Elisha Davis and his family were caught in a raging snowstorm that came out of nowhere. The weather had been perfect to start their journey, but now, it was a nightmare. None of them had gloves, thick coats, or thick socks. Somehow, he had to get his family out of this dangerous weather. If he didn't, they would all freeze to death.

Young Jonas grabbed his father's arm and shouted, "Daddy, I see a light over there!"
Elisha saw it too and shouted, "I see it, son. I smell

smoke, so let's head that way. Can you make it, Minnie?"

She replied, "I's can make it! Wes gots to git out of this weather!"

Elisha's heart jumped for joy when he realized it was indeed a house. The family stumbled up on the porch and collapsed at the front door. With every last ounce of energy Elisha had, he pounded on the door.

Ellen asked, "Did ya'll hear that noise at the front door?"

Teddy answered, "I heard it, Aunt Ellen."

Homer and Arthur grabbed their guns and got on each side of the door.

Jonas hit the door with his numb feet and yelled, "Help us!"

Homer opened the door and couldn't believe his eyes.

He shouted, "Help me git these folks inside, boys!"

The boys helped their fathers get the family inside by the fireplace. The ladies ran for blankets and dry clothes.

Arthur ordered, "We have to get these wet clothes off of them. We must work on their feet and hands to prevent frostbite, if we're not too late."

Poor Jonas kept begging, "Help us, please!"

Homer wrapped the boy in blankets and said, "Harry hold him in your arms real close, because he needs your body heat. Leann massage his feet in these warm cloths."

Ellen worked on Minnie and said, "Deidre hold her close while Grace works on her feet."

As Arthur wrapped Elisha in blankets, Teddy worked on his feet, and Ty held on to him.

Elisha pleaded, "Wes mean yous no harm, sir. Please help my wife and son."

Arthur replied, "We'll take care of you. Just rest and get warm. When was the last time you ate?"

"This morning, sir."

Kathleen commented, "I'll warm up food, fix biscuits, and warm lots of apple cider."

Little Andy walked over and laid down on Elisha. The folks couldn't help but laugh.

Arthur asked, "Why were you out in this dangerous snowstorm?"

Elisha answered, "The weather turned bad real quick, and wes couldn't see where wes was going."

Arthur asked, "Where were you going?"

"To the Yankee men across de river."

Homer remarked, "You could have died out there, man!"

"Then, wes would die free, sir."

Homer added, "There are Confederate soldiers between you and the Union army."

"We'll find a way to git across de river or die trying."

Homer acknowledged, "Well, I can't argue with that."

Arthur commented, "None of you are in any shape to walk to the river for a while."

"Wes doesn't want to be a burden on yous kind folks."

Homer scolded, "We believe in the Good Book. You needed help, so we did the right thing."

Lots of folks says they believe in de Good Book, but they doesn't live it. There bes lots of devil people in de churches."

Arthur agreed, "We know that kind. We aren't perfect, but we try to live right."

Minnie looked up with tears in her eyes and said, "Ya'll saved our lives! I's was sure we'd die in de snow. I's couldn't take another step."

Ellen replied, "Ya'll are safe, now. We'll get you nice and warm and get some food in you."

"Bless yous, ma'am. How is my boy?"

Ellen answered, "He's going to be fine."

Kathleen brought hot cider to the family to warm their bodies and souls. Later, the three were able to eat a hearty meal. All of them really enjoyed the honey biscuits.

Homer kept checking outside, and it was still snowing hard. He thought they must have at least a foot of snow with higher drifts.

Sleeping arrangements were made, and the fireplaces were roaring as the families snuggled and drifted off to sleep.

Many miles away from Caroline County the 47th Virginia soldiers huddled in their shanties trying to stay warm and wondering when it was going to stop snowing. At least, they weren't marching in it chasing the Yankee cavalry.

Winter quarters

David thought about his wife and son, "Were they safe?"

Clay wondered if the families had enough to eat, because the soldiers sure didn't. He hoped Ty and Harry were helping Homer run the farm and doing their share of the work?

Aaron thought about the terrible Christmas they spent in the Shenandoah Valley and wondered, "Would they defeat the Union army this year?"

Micah kept thinking about Grace and how soft her hair and lips felt. He had loved her before he was a teenager. He must survive this war, so he could marry her. He didn't want to see anymore horror, but he would do his duty to Virginia.

Gus thought about how much he missed his family and home. He wanted his life to get back to normal. Simply, he wanted to be a farmer.

He wondered, "Would he survive all the valleys of madness to come?"

Abner thought about the death of his brother, the home his parents were forced to leave, and how very tired he was. He was tired of killing, the war, and the destruction one could see across his beloved Virginia. He felt like an old man lost in the woods.

Ten days later, Elisha and his family left the Murphy farm loaded up with food and hopes for freedom. Even though the Murphy's had four sons fighting in the Rebel army, they would always be grateful for being saved from certain death. Somehow, Elisha's family had to get across the Rappahannock River to reach the Holy Grail of freedom.

Elisha had been to Fredericksburg before, so he guided his family west of the town. Carefully, they dodged Confederate encampments and picket lines until they found a good place to cross the river.

Homer had given Elisha some coffee to bribe a picket if need be to get across the river. Fortunately, he didn't need the coffee, because the picket had fallen asleep at his post.

Slowly with great care, the family slipped into the chilly water and crossed the river. Just as they got to shore and walked away from the river, a shot rang out and Jonas screamed in agony.

Elisha yelled, "Please massas, don't shot! We is runaway slaves! Please massas, my boy's hurt!"

The Union picket moved towards them and said, "Sweet Jesus man! I thought you was a Reb spy. I'm so sorry. Didn't you hear me tell you to stop and identify yourself?"

"No, massas! Please, help my boy!"

The picket ordered, "Follow me. I'll get you help! Can you carry him?"

"Yes, massas!"

The picket led them to a hospital tent where an orderly took Jonas and put him on a cot.

The orderly yelled, "Go get Dr. Hayden!"

Shortly, a tall, handsome man with blonde hair and blue eyes entered the tent and examined Jonas.

He asked, "What's your name, young man?"

"Jonas, massas."

Gabriel ordered, "Don't call me massas. Just call me sir or doc. You're free, now."

The doctor gave the orderly some instructions and said, "Jonas, I'll be right back after I talk to your parents over there."

The sentry told Gabriel, "I'm so sorry, sir. I didn't

know they were runaway slaves."

Gabriel replied, "Don't worry, private. The boy's going to be alright."

"Thank the Lord!"

Gabriel walked over to Elisha holding his weeping wife and said, "Jonas took a bullet in his thigh I need to remove. It didn't hit bone, so he's very lucky. Do I have your permission to operate on your son?"

Minnie replied with tears running down her cheeks, "Yes, massas, please save my boy!"

Gabriel reminded, "Don't call me massas. Just call me sir or doc."

Gabriel shook Elisha's hand and left to take care of Jonas. When the surgery was over, Jonas was moved to a bed in the hospital tent. Gabriel let Elisha and Minnie sit by his bed, so they'd be there when Jonas woke up.

Gabriel asked, "When was the last time you ate?"

Elisha answered, "Yesterday morning, sir."

The doctor told the orderly to get both of them a good meal.

Minnie asked, "How can wes ever repay yous for your kindness, sir?"

The doctor answered, "You don't need to."

Elisha remarked, "I's have to find work, so I's can take care of mys family."

Gabriel thought for a minute and suggested, "You could work for me. I need orderlies to help take care of my patients. I need help with laundry, feeding my patients, and cleaning my surgeon's uniforms and boots."

Elisha replied with excitement, "I's would like to be one of de orderlies, sir."

Minnie smiled and said, "I's can wash, cook, clean, and sew. I's can sew yous a shirt and anything else yous be a needin'."

Gabriel commented, "My surgeons and I will pay you well in Union money. Elisha, we'll train you to be an orderly. Minnie, we'll get you started bringing meals to the wounded and sick."

Elisha grinned and responded, "That's would be wonderful. Bless yous, sir!"

The doctor continued, "Eat a hearty meal and rest on these two cots next to Jonas. I'll make arrangements for a tent you can use. All of you will need extra clothing, so I'll take you over to the sutlers and get you set up with what you need, later."

Elisha asked, "How's can wes ever repay yous, sir?"

Gabriel answered, "Repay me by doing a good job, working hard, and being a good honest person."

Minnie added, "Wes make yous proud, sir!"

The doctor patted both of them on the shoulder and left to make his rounds.

On April 6th, the 47th Virginia marched to a clearing, formed up in ranks, and stood at attention in front of a soldier tied to a stake. The soldier had been found guilty of desertion and sentenced to be executed by firing squad. The soldier was from Company I, so the friends had to watch someone they knew die. Each man swallowed a knot in his throat when the order to fire came. They prayed to their maker for the man's soul and family. Why did he let his company down?

On April 21st, the regiment had to watch another soldier from Company G be executed for desertion. Company I had to form a firing squad to execute a deserter from the

55th Virginia. Most of the men thought it was an awful gut-wrenching sight.

Also, during April, the 47th Virginia's chaplain, Jacquelin Meredith, decided to resign and was replaced by Chaplain Samuel Barber.

On May 3rd, the men from Company I were saddened when Sgt John Watson died from pneumonia after battling several colds during the harsh winter in the Valley.

By May 1864, Gen A. P. Hill's corps went from 11,000 men to 22,000 men. Many soldiers had gotten back from illness, wounds, court martial punishments, or being exchanged. Many men exchanged by the Yankees didn't sign an oath not to fight against the Union, so they went back to their units. The 47th Virginia counted about 300 men fit for duty.

Early in May around the campfire, the friends were lost in thought about the upcoming campaign season.

David commented, "So, the Yankees have a new commander over Gen Meade."

Aaron added, "Ya, Lincoln thinks Gen Grant will defeat Gen Lee."

Gus blabbed, "That ain't going to happen. We'll push his behind into the Wilderness and beat on him until he gits fired."

Clay remarked, "He'll have to retreat back across the river like all the rest of them."

Micah went on, "Once we defeat Gen Grant and Lincoln loses the presidential election, the North will demand a peace treaty."

Abner suggested, "Let's end the war this year, so we

can all go home."

Pvt Ball responded, "That sounds like heaven to me."

David said, "I miss Sgt Watson, because he was a good man and a good sergeant."

Micah added, "All of us will miss our brothers in arms who aren't with us."

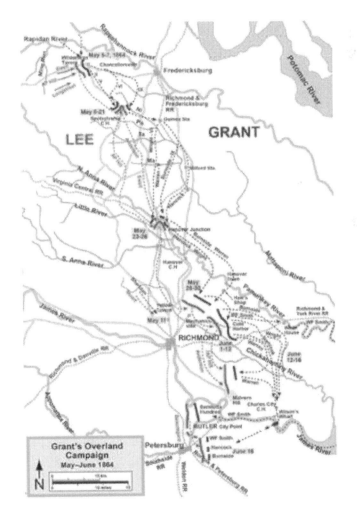

Gen Grant gathered almost 120,000 men to begin his Overland Campaign. He didn't target Richmond, but instead, Gen Lee's army. If he defeated Gen Lee's army of 64,000 men, Richmond would fall anyway. Gen Grant had no desire to fight a battle in the Wilderness. Soldiers couldn't see three yards in front of them. He wanted to fight on the open ground south and east of that dense underbrush, vines, and scrubby trees.

On the other hand, Gen Lee wanted to bottle up the Union army in the Wilderness.

On May 4th, the Union army started moving. The Union V Corps, VI Corps, and IX Corps crossed the Rapidan River using Germanna Ford. The Union II Corps crossed near Ely's Ford and marched towards Spotsylvania Court House. Gen Grant wanted his army to move quickly, but right away his plans started to unravel.

Gen Meade's supply trains, including over 4,000 wagons, 800 ambulances, and cattle for food, fell behind the corps. The army had to stop overnight, so the wagons could catch up.

Lee ordered Gen Ewell's II Corps at Morton's Ford to march eastward by way of the Orange Court House Turnpike. Gen A. P. Hill's III Corps and Lee's staff would march eastward by way of the Orange Plank Road. Gen Longstreet's I Corps was ordered from near Gordonsville to attack the Union flank like Gen Jackson had done a year ago at Chancellorsville.

The 47th Virginia marched about 12 miles on May 4th and stopped overnight near Mine Run. The following day Gen Heth's division made contact with Union forces not far from Widow Tapp's farm by early afternoon.

Gen Walker's brigade, including the 47th Virginia, was placed to the right of the Orange Plank Road next to a scrub forest near Brock Road. The 47th Virginia set up along a small ridge and put out a skirmish line.

By 4:00 pm, Gen Heth had ordered his division to attack.

Lt Embrey ordered Company I into battle line, and the line moved forward. The brigade came under furious fire and couldn't advance, so Walker's brigade moved their battle line below a slight mound. The men got busy placing every log they could find along that ridge for protection.

Clay gasped for breath and tried to control his emotions. His heart pounded in his head and throat. He drank from his canteen and made sure he had enough ammunition.

Aaron calmed himself down and wondered how many Union troops would be thrown at them.

Micah was calm, because he was one with his weapon. He knew he was a crack shot, and he was going to do everything in his power to get back to Grace.

A Vermont brigade charged the Confederate position and met a wall of bullets. Bullets were hitting trees and branches, so branches and leaves were falling like snow on the ground. The brigade suffered heavy losses and had to withdraw.

David wiped sweat and reloaded quickly.

He commented, "The Yankees will be back soon."

Abner shouted, "Here they come, boys!"

Aaron took aim at a Yankee soldier and pulled the trigger. The soldier dropped where he stood.

Gus focused on a corporal and fired. The blue soldier spun around and dropped.

Pvt Curtis yelled, "The Yanks are storming the

55th Virginia! They've broken the line."

Clay yelled, "Sweet Jesus, they've taken their flag!"

Sgt William Thompson from the 20th Indiana Infantry wrestled the flag from the wounded color bearer and was awarded the Medal of Honor for his gallantry. The following day he would be killed in action.

Lt Embrey ordered, "Fire low into their flank!"

The 47th Virginia and Gen Walker's other regiments shifted and poured deadly fire into the flanks of the enemy.

David aimed at a Yankee soldier, saw him go behind a tree, and waited for him to come out. The Union soldier took two steps and David fired. The soldier dropped into the tangled underbrush and disappeared.

David thought, "It's like hunting deer in this nightmare called the Wilderness."

Aaron heard Pvt James Bloxton yell, "I'm hit! Oh God, no!"

He grabbed James and saw he was shot in the right arm and hand. Aaron took a scarf off James and wrapped it around his wounded arm.

James pleaded, "I don't want to die! Don't leave me, Aaron! There's fires in this mess, and I don't want to burn up!"

Aaron said with a smile on his face, "You ain't going to die! Your arm's a flesh wound. We'll get you help as soon as we can."

The Union regiments fell back taking as many wounded back to their lines as they could.

Around 5:00 pm, another Union brigade charged Gen Walker's lines, but they were beaten back. Union

Gen Winfield Hancock's troops attacked Gen Walker's brigade four more times without success. The brigade was battered by almost 10,000 men, but they held their ground.

Gen A. P. Hill sent Gen Wilcox's brigade to relieve Gen Walker's boys, so they could go to the rear behind Wilcox's line. The men needed rest, ammunition, food, and the wounded taken where the hospitals were set up.

Aaron and David made sure Pvt Bloxton got to the field hospital, and then walked back to their line hoping they wouldn't collapse before they got there.

After nightfall, Gen Walker's brigade was ordered to the north side of the Orange Plank Road. They were told they would be relieved in the morning by Gen Longstreet's troops.

The smell of gunpowder hung heavily in the smoke filled air. Artillery shells exploded in various places in the Wilderness causing more fires.

The friends collapsed from pure exhaustion along with the other men in the brigade. Their faces and hands were black from gunpowder. Their eyes burned from the smoke, and their ears rang like church bells. They were a sorry looking bunch as they drifted off to sleep. They had no more adrenaline to keep them going. Like a spent bullet their bodies were spent, too.

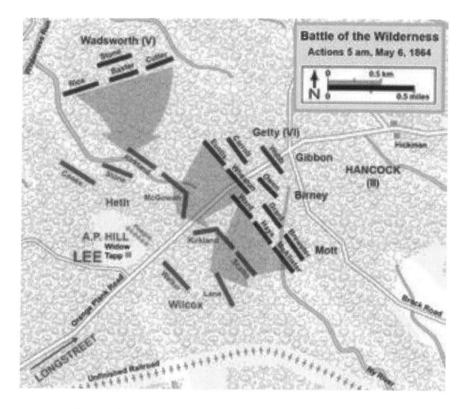

The men were jolted awake when Union Gen Hancock's II Corps attacked the Confederate lines at 5:00 am on May 6th. Tenaciously, the Rebel positions poured heavy fire into the blue columns. The brigade next to Gen Walker's position gave way and started to the rear. Without reinforcements the III Corps pulled out of their positions. As the friends were pulling back, an artillery shell exploded nearby. When Abner, Clay, David, and Micah regained consciousness, they all were sprawled in the dense thickets and trees. Clay was actually wrapped around a tree. Slowly, Clay rolled on his back and checked himself. He had a bloody nose, a gash on his head, one of his shoes was gone, and he didn't know where his musket was.

David had a bloody nose, his cheek was bleeding, he spit out a tooth, and his musket stock was gone.

Micah sat up, checked himself all over and only found some rips in his uniform. Other than some bruises and a few scratches he was fine. He saw Abner tangled up in a thicket with blood on his trousers. Micah crawled over to him and freed him. He checked Abner's leg and it was bad. A piece of shrapnel must have hit him.

David and Clay crawled over to Micah and knew right away Abner needed help soon.

Micah pleaded, "We have to get Abner to the surgeons fast!"

Clay cussed and remarked, "I have no idea where we are, let alone our regiment!"

Just then, the friends heard, "Come on boys, chase those Rebs all the way to Richmond."

The three friends pulled Abner way back into the thickets for cover while Micah held him in his arms.

He told the others, "If Abner comes to while the Yanks are around, we are dead meat. I'm putting my hand over his mouth just in case he wants to yell."

Clay whispered, "We have two muskets, two revolvers, and our knives. I ain't going to no Yank prison."

David suggested, "If they get too close, we can play opossum."

He smeared Micah's face with blood from his cheek wound.

The three friends quietly got their weapons ready. They had the element of surprise if the group was small enough. The Wilderness evened the odds, but it could also be a death trap. Fires were burning in several places, so there was no way to know how long this area would be safe. Fire could erupt anywhere.

The friends could hear branches snap under foot.

David thought, "Sweet Jesus, they're getting real close. Keep moving Yanks."

Clay's heart was pounding in his ears. He held a revolver close ready to fire at any time.

A Union soldier tripped, fell, and started cussing a blue streak telling the state of Virginia what it could do to itself.

Just then, Abner started to regain consciousness.

Micah whispered in his ear, "Yankees are real close. Don't yell or make a sound. Easy Abner, don't move."

Abner was suffering in agony. Tears ran down Micah's hand, so he knew Abner was suffering the hinges of hell.

An artillery shell exploded several yards away, and one of the Yankees started cussing.

The soldier shouted, "Don't the artillery fools know we're chasing Rebs in this god forsaken patch of ground?"

Another Yank asked, "How you know it wasn't a Rebel artillery shell?"

He answered, "I know the difference."

"You're full of bull, too!"

Micah whispered, "Hang in there, Abner. I know you hurt real bad."

Micah could feel Abner quiver in his arms. When were the Yanks going to leave?

Clay caught sight of three Yanks. Where were the rest of them? He signaled David and Micah with three fingers and their location.

Suddenly, a frightened deer burst out of the underbrush in front of the four friends. Pow! Pow! Pow!

Clay heard the hiss of a bullet flash past him. Another shot buried itself in a tree nearby. The third shot grazed David's arm, but he couldn't yell, cuss, or call for help.

They heard a soldier yell, "Come on you three. We got to get out of here."

Clay noticed the smoke was getting thicker. They had to get out of this tangled prison. The fires must be getting closer, because the Yanks were gone, now. The friends were running out of options.

David stated, "I'm not burning to death in these thickets!"

Clay chimed in, "I'm not going to some Yankee prison to die!"

Micah went on, "We fight our way out or die trying!"

Clay asked, "Abner, what do you say?"

Weakly, he answered, "We fight!"

Micah told Abner, "Put your arms around my neck, and I'll carry you on my back."

Slowly, the group got up and helped Abner onto Micah's back. The smoke was getting thicker, and the boys could hear men scream for mercy.

Clay led the group, so he could cut through the tangled thicket. Bless Judge Murphy for giving them these priceless knives. Every step was a struggle to get through the vines and underbrush.

Micah told Abner, "I bet all of us are full of chiggers."

Abner replied, "I don't want them setting up house in my behind."

Micah chuckled and agreed.

Suddenly, Clay heard someone yell, "Please help me!"

There in front of him was a Union soldier shot in both legs.

He pleaded, "I don't want to die in this raging inferno. Help me or shoot me."

David asked Clay, "Do you think you can carry him?"

"Ya, but can you cut through this mess with one arm?"

David replied, "It's a flesh wound, so I can manage."

David helped the Yank get on Clay's back, and the group kept moving away from the thick smoke.

Suddenly, David came across a small path, and he knew where he was. He had been hunting with his boss several times using the path. There were the two trees that had fallen and made a X. If they turned left, it would take them where they needed to go. Now, they could make better time, because they didn't have to cut their way out.

The further they went the less smoke was hanging in the air.

David said, "We're almost out of this mess, Abner. Hang in there a little longer."

The group broke out of the thickets onto clear ground. However, where was the 47th Virginia and the help they needed? They knew they had to walk towards the sound of the musket fire. They decided to walk along the edge of the thickets, so they could duck back inside for protection if need be.

The Yank said, "If we find Rebel troops first, I'll be your prisoner. The war's over for me."

Clay responded, "Our surgeons will treat you right."

David asked, "What happens if we run into Yankee

troops?"

The Yank answered, "Put me down on the open ground, duck back into the thickets, and get away."

It wasn't long before they knew one heck of a fight was going on. The group caught sight of some Texas flags and knew Gen Longstreet's I Corps had arrived on the battlefield.

The group ducked back in the thickets, because bullets were flying everywhere. The artillery was firing shells a little too close, so they all knew they'd be better off in the thickets lying low. If they stayed in the open some sharpshooter was bound to shoot them dead as a chicken with no head.

The friends were right. Gen Longstreet's advanced troops reached the battlefield in time to stop the Union onslaught. A brigade of 800 Texans pitched into Gen Hancock's boys along with two more brigades and drove the Yankee troops passed the Widow Tapp farm. The Texans paid a monumental ransom for stopping the collapse of the Confederate army. They suffered 550 casualties for their act of gallantry.

Gen Heth was able to rally his division and had them entrench north of the Orange Plank Road.

Gen A. P. Hill couldn't perform his duty as commander of the III Corps, because he was very ill. Gen Jubal Early was given command of the III Corps.

Another corps commander fell when Gen Longstreet was shot in the neck by his own men. Command of the I Corps was given to Gen Richard Anderson.

The group was now in Confederate held positions, so

they carefully moved out of the thickets. They were never so glad to see motley gray uniforms in their entire lives.

They grabbed stretcher-bearers for Abner and the Yank. An orderly set the men down to clean their wounds and bandaged them. They were sore, hungry, and exhausted. They were sure the last two days had been ten years long.

The men ate, found a place to sleep, and fell into a deep exhaustive sleep. Tomorrow, they would check on Abner and report back to their regiment. They wondered what tomorrow would be like compared to today.

Abner was spinning in a fog not knowing where he was. Everything was getting brighter, and he stopped spinning. He saw his brother, Richard, walking towards him. His brother looked so happy.

Richard reached out his hand and said, "I've come to get you, Abner. Take my hand and you will find peace, love, no sorrow and no pain. It is your time to leave this horror and come home."

Abner asked, "Am I dying?"

"Yes, you must pass on, so you can find eternal peace."

Abner kept reaching until he touched his brother's hand and looked into his eyes. It was then that he felt the grace of God.

The fellers walked into the hospital tent looking for Abner. They stopped an orderly and asked about their friend.

The orderly answered, "I'm sorry, but your friend died about fifteen minutes ago. He just lost too much blood."

Micah shouted in anger, "Where is he?"

"We put him behind the tent with the other dead until we have time to bury them."

Micah, Clay, and David raced out of the tent and frantically searched for their beloved friend. When they found him, Micah took Abner's knife to return to his family and started pounding the ground with his fists.

"No, no, no, not Abner! You already took Richard! His family will be devastated! Not Abner!"

Micah kept pounding the ground with his fists while he wept on his knees.

David and Clay knelt next to him while tears ran down their bloodied and bruised faces.

Finally, David asked, "Did you look at Abner's face?"

"No! All I saw was his knife and hands."

David explained, "He had such a peaceful smile on his face. He's in a lot better place than we are. Let's pick a place to bury him, mark it well, and when this madness is over we'll come back for him."

"Give me a little more time, and then, we'll bury him."

Burying Abner was the hardest thing they had ever done. Sure, they buried lots of dead soldiers from so many other battlefields, but he was like a brother to them. All of them had such good times together and had walked through the Valley of Madness together. There would be an empty place in their hearts, because he was gone. How were they going to tell his parents?

The 47th Virginia suffered twenty casualties during the Battle of the Wilderness. Among the dead would be Pvt Robert Brown from Co. A and Pvt Woodford Loving from Co. E.

The two armies had battered each other and piled up tremendous casualties. The Union lost over 17,500 men while the Confederacy lost over 11,000 men they couldn't replace.

Gen Grant decided not to attack Gen Lee's well entrenched positions. The last thing he wanted to do was fight in the Wilderness after last year's battle at Chancellorsville. He would sidestep Lee's army, move to the southeast, and get between Gen Lee and Richmond.

When the Union soldiers learned they weren't retreating, their morale soared. They were tired of crossing the Rappahannock River defeated. Each man knew they could fight Gen Lee's army, because they had done it at Gettysburg. Maybe, this Gen Grant was willing to slug it out like a boxer in a street fight.

Gen U. S. Grant

Faces of the Civil War

CHAPTER 8

David, Clay, and Micah got back to their regiment much to the relief of Aaron and Gus. All were saddened by the death of Abner Moss, because they knew it could have been one of them.

The regiment spent May 7th waiting for the Yankees to attack, again.

On the nights of May 7th and May 8th, Gen Grant divided his army and ordered them to march ten miles to Spotsylvania Court House. Two of his corps would use the Orange Plank Road, and his other two corps would use Brock Road.

Gen A. P. Hill's III Corps, commanded by Gen Jubal Early, including the 47th Virginia, was ordered to Spotsylvania Court House. Gen Lee wanted to beat Grant's forces to the crossroads to keep Grant from getting between him and Richmond.

The corps camped at Shady Grove on May 8th and marched to the crossroads by May 9th.

The Confederate army spent the nights of May 8th and May 9th building formidable earthworks about four miles long from the Po River to Brock Road. The center of this line jutted out about a mile to resemble a mule shoe.

On May 10th, Gen Early's troops were ordered to engage Union forces west of Spotsylvania Court House that were trying to hit Gen Lee's flank. At Talley's Mill, Gen Heth's division pitched into Gen Hancock's II Corps and drove them back to the Po River. Gen Hancock pulled all his divisions north of the Po River except one. This division was pulling back when Gen Heth pitched into them around 2:30 pm. His first two attacks failed, so Gen Heth tried a third time.

Clay shouted, "Our artillery shells have started fires in the woods the Yankees have to go through before they get to the Po River!"

Aaron yelled, "The Yanks better run mighty fast to get to the river."

Gus added, "Them Yanks are sure putting up a fight!"

Now, that most of the Rebel soldiers had rifled muskets, they could hit a target 300 yards away.

Several men were shot before they could run the gauntlet to the river. Many of the Union troops burned to death in the woods before they could cross the river.

David saw Pvt Nathaniel Ball fall next to him shot in the chest. Gen Walker was shot in the foot. The Confederate ranks held their positions, and then tended to their wounded. Unfortunately, Gen Walker had his foot amputated and was lost to the brigade.

Even though Col Mayo was under court martial, he was given command of the brigade. Lt Col John Lyell ended up commanding the 47th Virginia.

The night of May 11th the area was hit by a severe rainstorm. The rain pounded the men, ground, and ammunition.

Gus complained, "I feel like I'm standing in a well."

Aaron asked, "Are you sure it isn't a waterfall?"

Clay chimed in, "I'd say both."

David added, "This confounded rain is going to wet

our gunpowder."

Micah responded, "The Yanks will have the same problem."

Aaron replied, "We might end up clubbing each other to death."

Gus fired back, "Thanks for that wonderful thought."

For some strange reason, the friends giggled at that stupid exchange of thoughts.

Col Mayo's brigade was sent to support Poague's artillery located not quite a mile north of the courthouse. The battalion was positioned on an outwardly projecting point in the Confederate line. Mayo's brigade took up position between Gen Archer's brigade on the left and Gen Lane's brigade on the right. The rest of Gen Heth's division was sent to reinforce the Confederate position attacked by Gen Hancock's II Corps. The area would become known as the "Bloody Angle."

Mayo's brigade was located on the east side of the "Mule Shoe." The men looked out on an open area and behind that was dense pine trees and thickets. The brigade put out a skirmish line in the pines. It started to rain around 8:00 am.

Civil War tent

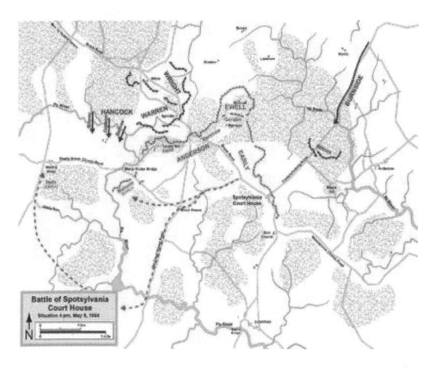

Around 9:00 am, Gen Burnside's IX Corps attacked. The skirmish line raised the alarm as Burnside's three battle ranks headed right at Mayo's troops. The Confederate artillery fired grape and canister shells at the blue ranks.

Gus became one with his musket firing one aimed shot after another. Their fortifications helped protect them while the Yankees were sitting ducks out in the open.

Each friend could fire, rapidly. They weren't fumbling recruits anymore, but seasoned shooters.

Clay shouted, "The Yanks are pulling back to the trees! They're stupid to attack us in the rain!"

David commented, "Gen Lee's headquarters is close by, so we have to hold our position no matter what happens."

Aaron shouted, "Here they come, again!"

Micah yelled, "Didn't the Yanks learn anything from Pickett's Charge?"

Lt Embrey yelled, "Pour fire into them, boys!"

Gus took aim and fired at a corporal trying to step over a dead comrade. He fell shot in the chest.

Canister sprayed the ranks as groups of men fell dead or wounded. The wounded begged for mercy.

Clay was sprayed with blood and flesh, he turned, and saw Lt Embrey fall to the bottom of the muddy trench.

"Lieutenant, you hit bad?"

When Clay checked him, he knew he was dead. Clay reloaded quickly and fired. The Union ranks fell back to the woods leaving piles of wounded and dead behind. What a horrible, gruesome sight was left in front of the salient. Many wounded were lying under the dead and couldn't free themselves from their tombs.

Fighting at other parts of the Confederate line was like a blood-curdling frenzy of horror. Blood flowed down the sides of the trenches to the muddy goo at the bottom.

At times, fighting was reduced to murderous hand-to-hand combat. Both sides endured close to 24 hours of savage combat.

Gen Lee's engineers frantically built a new defensive earthworks south of the Mule Shoe.

On May 13th, the hungry, exhausted Rebel soldiers moved to the new earthworks.

David looked around dumbfounded and said, "Everything is flattened. The trees, leaves, and bushes are gone."

Gus remarked, "I've never seen anything like it. Larger trees are blown to bits or sawed off by musket fire."

Clay complained, "I wish it would stop raining, so we can cook our rations."

David asked, "Why hasn't Gen Grant asked for a truce to save his wounded and bury his dead?"

Aaron responded, "His dead are rotting all over the

battlefield. The stench is horrible. It's bad enough to gag a horse!"

Micah asked, "Do you think Gen Grant will attack today?"

Clay answered, "If he doesn't, he might move again like he did at the Wilderness."

Gus suggested, "Gen Lee will beat him wherever Grant goes."

David explained, "It's rained so much the roads must be nothing but a quagmire like quicksand."

Micah replied, "Reminds me of the swamps on the Peninsula."

Bloody Angle

In the trenches, the Confederates stood in mud, wore wet clothes, and couldn't cook their rations. Finally, the men received rations on May 17th and ate their fill even though the rotting corpses were putting off a horrible stench.

The 47th Virginia suffered nine casualties.
Lt Richard Embrey from Co. I was killed in action and
Pvt Thomas Grymes from Co. G was mortally wounded
in action.

During the Battle of Spotsylvania Court House,
Confederate casualties were between 10,000 to 13,000
men. Gen Grant's Union forces suffered around 18,000
casualties. To make matters worse for Grant, another
20,000 men's enlistments were up, so they left to return
home. Gen Grant pulled troops from the heavy artillery
units manning the various forts around Washington,
D. C. Veteran regiments referred to these units as band
box regiments with new uniforms and clean equipment.
They were living the good life in the capital. The
veterans were sure these units would run at the sound
of the first bullets fired. These regiments would be like
raw recruits. Also, Grant pulled Gen Baldy Smith's
XVIII Corps from the Army of the James.

During the Battle of Spotsylvania Court House, five
general officers were mortally wounded or killed in
action.

The 47th Virginia left the horrible stench of unburied
corpses on May 21st and marched 11 miles to Mitchell's
Shop. The following day they marched in the
oppressive heat south of the North Anna River.
Gen Heth's division built fortifications south of the river
near Anderson's Station.

Gen Grant decided not to attack the Confederate
fortified trenches, so he slid his army to the left and
southward.

Gen Lee with the help of President Jefferson Davis

pulled the division of Gen Robert Hoke from below the James River. The division numbered over 7,000 men. They started arriving on May 31st.

Likewise, Gen Grant's reinforcements started arriving at White House Landing on May 30th. Union troops would number close to 108,000 men, but many of these men were not battle tested veterans.

Gen Lee's forces by June 1st would number around 59,000 men.

Col Birkett Fry was promoted to brigadier general and given command of Col Mayo's brigade. Fry had already been captured and wounded four times in battle, so the men respected his leadership.

Gen Birkett Fry

The two armies kept maneuvering until fate placed them on familiar ground. The Battle of Cold Harbor 1864 would be fought near Gaines's Mill. The two armies fought each other here during the Peninsula Campaign of 1862. The area was about ten miles from the Confederate capital.

Gen Grant could receive supplies and reinforcements from the Pamunkey River. He was close enough to attack Richmond or pitch into Gen Lee's army.

Lee's Army of Northern Virginia got busy digging entrenchments with barricades of logs. They built zigzagging lines inside of lines from the Chickahominy River on the right to the Totopotomay River on the left. Artillery was placed, so they could fire on multiple positions. The trenches were a maze to make it difficult for the Union forces to determine how many troops were in front of them.

On June 1st, Gen Heth's division relieved Gen Early's division near Totopotomay Creek. This put them on the left flank of the army.

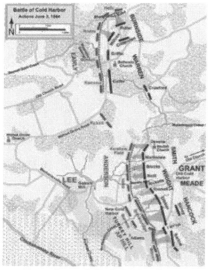

Battle of Cold Harbor

During the evening, they skirmished with some Union troops and sent them running.

The following evening Gen Heth's and Gen Rodes's divisions charged the Union troops in front of them and captured many of Gen Burnside's men.

Many Union soldiers wrote their names on paper and pinned the paper inside their uniform jackets, because they knew what an attack against fortified entrenchments meant. Rank after rank of them would be mowed down one on top of the other. The wounded would be left behind to die and rot on the battlefield in the oppressive heat just like at Spotsylvania Court House.

June 3rd would be one of the most horrific days fought during the Civil War. Gen Grant sent his corps on a frontal assault towards the Confederate lines. Even a ground fog added to the feeling of doom among the Union soldiers.

The Confederate soldiers all along the maze of trenches poured volley after volley into the blue ranks. Some wore faded uniforms while others wore new uniforms as if they were on parade.

The artillery poured canister shell after shell into the attacking blue ranks. It reminded many of the Confederate soldiers of the Union attacks on Marye's Heights during the Battle of Fredericksburg.

On the left flank of the Confederate line, Gen Heth's and Gen Rodes's divisions poured volley after volley into the Union ranks during two assaults. Union Gen Burnside's forces were unable to break through the Rebel fortifications.

Fry's brigade, including the 47th Virginia, were at the end of the line. Union cavalry attacked the end hoping to roll it up and get behind the Rebel lines.

Cpl Steptoe Washington had been exchanged in March from a Union prison.

He yelled, "Drop the horses! Fix bayonets!"

David looked at the surreal scene as horses and riders galloped towards the maze of trenches.

He thought, "I love horses. How can I shoot one that's not injured?"

He aimed at a rider, waited for the best shot, and fired. The rider jerked back, fell from the horse, but his foot got caught in the stirrup. The horse veered off to the right in a frightened frenzy.

Aaron fired at another rider, but missed. A few seconds later, both rider and horse dropped.

Gus took a deep breath, wiped sweat from his eyes, and fired. Another rider dropped to the ground.

Clay's mouth was like cotton, and it was hard to breathe. He aimed, fired, and the horse dropped. The rider got to his feet, fired his revolver, and launched himself over the logs. Micah took his knife, grabbed the soldier, and buried the knife in the throat.

Another Union cavalryman jumped Sgt Augustus Patton, but Gus buried his bayonet into the Yankee's back.

All along the brigade's line, the same thing was happening until the cavalry was ordered to fall back.

Then, infantry charged the flank, but they were beaten back.

The friends panted, wiped sweat, and drank as much water as they could. They were hot, hungry, and exhausted. The boys always felt this way after an intense fight. They were all simply drained of energy.

They made sure their muskets were reloaded in case there was another attack. They waited, but another assault never came.

Cpl Steptoe shouted, "Hot dang, we held the end of the line!"

When the men calmed down, Micah asked, "I wonder how many mosquitoes we killed today?"

David asked, "Are you cotton picking serious?"

Aaron chimed in, "I'd say about a thousand."

Gus complained, "Too bad we can't eat them."

Clay remarked, "Too bad we can't eat these confounded, ornery beetles!"

David asked, "I wonder how they'd taste cooked over a campfire?"

Pvt John J. Jones added, "I'm so hungry I could eat one raw."

Aaron asked, "How did we get off on this stupid topic?"

Gus suggested, "Blame Micah!"

Micah continued, "I can't believe I crapped in my pants!"

Clay commented, "I can't believe I peed in mine!"

The group giggled, even though there wasn't anything funny about this hellish place. Their minds needed to concentrate on something else to help them keep their sanity.

Cpl Steptoe said, "Guess what I just found off a couple of dead horses?"

David replied, "Let me guess. You found some horse

manure."

"No, saddle bags with food in them."

The friends gathered around to enjoy hardtack, candy, canteens full of water, honey, and biscuits. To the group this was Thanksgiving Day in June.

Cold Harbor earthworks

On June 4th, Gen Heth's division marched all the way from the left flank of the Rebel line to the right flank of the army. The men suffered badly in the filthy maze of trenches with little food or clean water.

Those who suffered the most were the wounded between the lines. They begged for water and mercy.

Micah said in anger, "I can't stand this! I'm going to take water to some of these poor devils!"

Cpl Steptoe shouted, "No, you don't! A sharpshooter will kill you before you get out of the trench. Besides, we don't have enough water to spare."

Micah asked, "Why doesn't Grant ask for a truce?"

Cpl Steptoe answered, "Because that would be admitting defeat."

Finally, by June 7th, a truce was arranged. However, very few wounded were still alive. The dead were baked black from the sun and decomposing, so many were buried where they died.

The 47th Virginia suffered eleven casualties at Cold Harbor. The following men were killed or mortally wounded in action:
Pvt Walter Heflin KIA
Pvt Robert Sutton MWIA
Capt Clarence Woolfolk KIA
Pvt Cornelius Rose MWIA
Pvt William Bendall KIA
Pvt Charles Yates KIA

Finally, on June 13th, the men climbed out of the filthy maze of trenches and got ready to march. They were more than glad to be above the ground and away from the stench of death and the army of beetles feasting on the dead. All of them wondered if they would ever be clean, again.

Beetles

Cold Harbor would add many more casualties to both sides. The Union suffered around 13,000 killed, wounded, and captured compared to Confederate losses around 5,000 men. Union casualties would have been much less if Gen Grant hadn't ordered the assaults on June 3rd.

Northern newspapers blasted Gen Grant's handling of the Battle of Cold Harbor. Northern families were outraged at the casualty lists, and an anti-war movement was gaining momentum. Some northern cities such as New York were having to deal with draft riots.

The Confederacy hoped that these events would affect the upcoming presidential election. If Lincoln lost the election, the Confederate government was confident the North would pursue a peace treaty.

Gen Grant decided he was in another stalemate with Gen Lee, so he put together another plan to force Lee to pull some of his forces away from Gen Grant's front. He sent Gen Philip Sheridan to the Shenandoah Valley to destroy as much of the Virginia Central Railroad tracks around Charlottesville as he could. Union forces in the Valley were making good progress destroying supplies meant for Gen Lee's army. The Shenandoah Valley was the bread basket for Gen Lee's army. If Gen Grant could stop this food supply, Gen Lee's army would be in serious trouble.

Lastly, Gen Grant decided to cross the James River and go after Petersburg. The city was a railroad and road junction that connected the Lower South and other parts of the state. If Gen Grant could capture these railroad lines, he could deny Gen Lee's army the food and supplies they needed to continue the fight. Of course, this also meant the civilian population would suffer, too. The meaning of total war would become crystal clear to the South in the coming months.

Faces of the Civil War

CHAPTER 9

Between the Battle of Spotsylvania Court House and Cold Harbor, the Murphy families would experience a taste of total warfare.

The family was eating their noon meal when they heard a lot of musket fire in the distance. The men and Ellen grabbed their weapons and everyone got away from the windows after closing the shutters. They knew there was serious fighting going on west of Fredericksburg. They had no idea if it was infantry, cavalry, or how close it was.

Homer ordered, "I have no idea where the bullets are flying, so everyone stay down."

Ty asked, "Do you want me to go to the barn?"

"No! I don't want you hit by a stray bullet."

Arthur commented, "Maybe, it won't last long. It could be a small skirmish going on."

"Let's hope so."

For what seemed like four days, the firing finally stopped. The family waited a while longer, and then, Homer saw Yankee cavalry bearing down on the house. The cavalry surrounded the house, and an officer and two privates pounded on the front door.

The lieutenant yelled, "Everybody out or we'll burn the house and barn!"

Arthur suggested, "Now is no time for guns. We don't want to give them an excuse to shoot or burn."

Homer answered, "I agree."

They put their weapons away and slowly opened the

door.

Homer yelled, "Don't shoot! We're unarmed! I have women and children inside!"

The lieutenant yelled, "Git out on the porch, now!"

The women and children clung to each other terrified. Ellen cautioned them to stay calm and be quiet. The last thing they needed was a smart mouth to rile up the pig-headed Yankees.

Homer asked, "What's wrong, Lieutenant?"

"Reb cavalry ambushed my men before they high-tailed it. Git the Rebs out of your house and barn!"

Homer replied, "There ain't no soldiers in my house or barn. Go ahead and search if you like."

The lieutenant shouted, "Private, git that gal and check inside! Corporal, git that gal and check the barn! If Rebs are around, the girls are dead!"

Arthur warned, "Do not harm one hair on our girl's heads."

The lieutenant answered, "We'll jest see about that."

The Union soldiers searched both, but found no Rebel soldiers.

Homer asked, "Can I offer you and your men some apple cider?"

"No! We'll fill our canteens at the well."

One private commented, "There's biscuits, honey, and ham on the table, lieutenant."

The officer ordered, "Two of you women bring my men a plate of food. They're starving."

Ellen answered, "Don't worry, we won't cause any trouble."

The officer asked a private, "How many horses are in

the barn and grazing?"

"Six, sir."

The officer ordered, "We'll take three!"

Homer reminded, "Lieutenant, we need those horses to plow and pull wagons."

"The Union cavalry needs horses. We lost two horses, because you Rebs killed them! Don't argue!"

Ty spoke up and pleaded, "Please, sir, don't take Blackie, because he's our best horse!"

Homer thought, "What is that fool boy up to? Blackie was an ornery, mean, and crazy horse. The first Yankee that got on him would end up in Richmond."

The private remarked, "That be a fact. Well, I know he'll be a comin' with us."

Ty burst into tears as Homer said, "Don't mind my boy, sir. Blackie is his favorite."

The private grinned and replied, "Too bad, boy!"

Ellen and Deidre gave the cavalrymen the food and watched them gobble it down in a hurry. Both women prayed Teddy would stay in the woods until the Yanks were gone. Teddy was fishing in hopes of bringing dinner home. His father told him to stay hidden in the woods if he ever heard musket fire or saw Yankees around.

Teddy had a great morning fishing with plenty to show for it. When the musket fire started, he scrambled up in his tree house and hid. When the firing stopped, he waited a while, and then, climbed down. When he got close to the tree line, he was grabbed from behind and a large hand clamped over his mouth.

"I'm not going to hurt you, boy. There's Yankee

cavalry at the house. So far, they haven't hurt your family. You have to stay here until the Yanks have skedaddled."

Teddy nodded, and the Rebel soldier slowly removed his hand.

Teddy asked, "Are they going to kill my folks?"

"I don't know."

Teddy asked, "Did you fight the Yanks, earlier?"

"Yep, we kilt some, but they outnumbered us, so we had to split up to get away."

Teddy said, "Your pants and leg are all bloody."

"Ya, I took a bullet. It's just a flesh wound."

Teddy suggested, "You need help. Our women folk can help you. I'll try to get you to our house."

"We have to stay put until the Yanks leave."

Teddy asked, "Where's your horse?"

"He's somewhere in these woods. It was too painful to ride him."

Teddy said in anger, "The Yanks are stealing some of our horses!"

"There's nothin' we can do about it, now. When they start stealing things, it won't be long before they leave."

Teddy asked, "What's your name?"

"Zebulon Carter. What's yours?"

"Teddy Murphy."

"It looks like the Yanks are stealing some chickens, too."

"I hope they choke on a chicken bone and drop stone dead."

"Amen to that, Teddy."

Teddy suggested, "You're bleeding a lot. I'm going to wrap my shirt around your leg real good."

"Thanks, that will make it feel better. Looks like the Yanks are moving out."

"It's about time!"

"We'll stay hidden a while longer. Then, you can go for help."

The two waited about fifteen minutes, and Teddy took off for the house. He threw open the door and frightened the bejesus out of everybody inside.

Teddy shouted, "Poppa, you got to help a wounded soldier in the woods!"

Homer ordered, "Take a deep breath, Teddy. Now, start at the beginning."

His leg is real bad. He stopped me and warned me about the Yankees. You got to help him, Uncle Homer!"

Homer and Arthur grabbed their weapons and took off after Teddy followed by Ty and Harry. While Teddy was gone, the Rebel soldier's horse came back to Zebulon.

Teddy pointed, "He's over there by the thick bushes!"

Arthur and Homer knelt beside the soldier and examined his leg.

Teddy added, "His name's Zebulon Carter."

Harry asked, "What's in the bag?"

Teddy answered, "Oh, I forgot! It's full of fish for dinner."

Homer asked, "Well, Zebulon, can we move you to the house?"

"Yes, sir."

"We'll get you up, wrap your arms around our necks, and we'll help carry you."

"Bless you, sir."

Homer suggested, "Take his horse to the barn, Ty, and give him food and water."

"Yes, sir!"

Arthur asked, "Is this your shirt, Teddy?"

"Yes, sir."

"You did a good thing, son."

Homer and Arthur got the soldier inside the house and laid him on a pallet Ellen had put together.

Zebulon remarked, "Take my horse, sir. He'll replace one of your stolen horses. There are three dead Yankees and two of our men near your wagon road to the south."

Arthur responded, "We'll take care of your horse until you mend."

Homer and Ellen removed Teddy's shirt and took a real close look at the wound. Teddy held the soldier's hand while Ellen cleaned the wound.

Zebulon squeezed Teddy's hand and said, "I want you to keep my sword. I have no one to give it to."

"Ain't you married, sir?"

"No wife and no children."

Teddy asked, "What about your parents?"

"Both of them died this past winter from pneumonia."

Homer commented, "Zebulon, there ain't no doctor in these parts. Where's the army doctors?"

"Both armies pulled out of Spotsylvania Court House a few days ago and are heading south."

Ellen continued, "That means the Yankees will be crawling all over this area."

"We were following the Yanks to see where the army was heading."

Arthur asked, "We have sons fighting with the 47th Virginia Infantry. Are they close by?"

"I don't think so."

Zebulon looked at Teddy and said, "You're a fine, young man."

The soldier looked into Teddy's eyes, winked, smiled, and took his last breath. His face turned an ashen white.

Tears ran down Teddy's face as he pleaded, "You can't die!"

Homer added, "His leg was real bad, and he lost a lot of blood. He's not suffering anymore, Teddy."

"He was my best friend!"

Teddy put his head on Zebulon's chest and wept. Arthur knew Teddy needed some time to deal with the soldier's death. His son had a tender heart and soul. His feelings ran deeper than most folks.

Arthur slipped out to the barn, got Zebulon's sword, and brought it back to the house. He handed the sword to Teddy, and the boy held it tightly as tears continued to roll down his cheeks.

A while later, Arthur suggested, "Teddy, help me pick out a special place to bury Zebulon."

"Can we bury him on the hill, so he can watch over our house?"

Ellen answered, "I think that's a fine place. We'll wrap him up real nice."

Leann asked, "Do you want his cap and pocket watch, Teddy?"

"Yes, if Harry doesn't want it."

The men dug Zebulon's grave, and Homer read from the Good Book. Arthur said a prayer and stepped away, so Teddy could say goodbye. It was strange how Teddy felt such a kinship to the soldier. They must have been kindred spirits.

Once Zebulon was buried, the men and boys took

their wagon down the road to look for the other dead. Sure enough, there were the three dead Yankees and two dead Confederate cavalrymen.

Harry spoke up and said, "There's a Yankee horse next to the tree line."

Homer suggested, "Harry, go over there real gentle like and get him. Looks like he's alright."

Harry brought the horse back and tied him to the wagon.

Arthur commented, "It looks like he's your horse now, Harry."

Homer remarked, "Arthur, it looks like these Yanks have some mighty fine boots on."

Arthur smiled and responded, "I think I can wear this poor devil's boots."

He tried them on, and they were a perfect fit. Homer found a pair that fit him, but the third pair was too big for any of the boys. They'd keep them, because the boys would grow into them.

Ty and Harry took the soldiers' swords and put them in the wagon. Homer kind of figured each boy wanted one.

Homer commented to Arthur, "The Confederate cavalrymen are very thin, their uniforms are worn out, and their boots are pitiful. I pray our sons don't look like this."

Arthur agreed and said, "If all our soldiers look like this, then the Confederacy is in trouble. If we can't feed and supply our army, the South will not win."

Homer went on, "I'm thinking the same thing."

The men and boys took the wagon back behind the house and buried the five cavalrymen. Arthur said a few words over their graves and left.

Ty and Harry took the horses back to the barn and unhitched the wagon.

Teddy and Grace cleaned the fish, because they were going to fry fish for dinner.

Homer commented in the house, "I felt like a thief taking things from the dead, but they didn't need the items."

Ty reminded, "Clay and Gus said they took stuff from the dead all the time."

Homer replied, "That's right! Then, I'm not going to feel bad about it, neither."

Harry added, "Me, neither!"

Teddy looked at Harry and thought, "Your sword doesn't mean much to you, but my sword is precious to me."

Leann confided to Grace, "I was scared to death the Yankees were going to burn our home and barn to the ground."

Grace responded, "I was terrified they'd kill us!"

Deidre replied, "All I could think about was how the Yankees looted and burned Fredericksburg. Shoot fire, they even looted the Baptist Church!"

Kathleen went on, "I didn't like the way some of those Yankees were looking at us. They had that rape look on their faces."

Ellen chimed in, "If any soldier tries to rape one of you girls, I'll beat their heads in with my iron frying pan."

The ladies couldn't help but giggle. They knew when Ellen got mad she could beat the crap out of anybody.

Ellen was not above playing dirty, fighting dirty, and enjoying every minute of the brawl. She'd turn one of those Yankees inside out in twenty seconds and not break a sweat. She could pour on the southern belle charm, or strike a person like a cottonmouth snake. Sometimes a woman had to do what she had to do. Even if she looked like she walked through a tornado, Ellen didn't care. She could go to church the next Sunday and ask for forgiveness.

Faces of the Civil War

CHAPTER 10

Three days after the cavalry skirmish, Leann went to the barn to get some feed for the chickens. When she got near the feed, she stopped dead in her tracks, screamed, and rushed to the house.

She threw open the door and started crying.

Ellen demanded, "Sweet Jesus, child! What's wrong with you?"

"Hurry, there's something bad wrong in the barn!"

Kathleen asked, "What's wrong?"

Leann ran out the front door like a crazy woman with her bloomers on fire.

Ellen grabbed her gun, because all the men were in the fields working. Kathleen and Deidre grabbed their revolvers and followed Leann. Grace stayed behind to take care of little Andy.

Ellen looked where Leann was pointing and just about fainted. Now was time for quick action and a cool head. All of them could fall apart later.

Ellen knelt down next to the young woman and felt for a pulse, but there was none. The poor thing was dead, and next to her was a newborn crying, softly.

Ellen ordered Kathleen, "You know what I need. Run and get it, girl! We got to cut the cord, clean the baby up, and feed it!"

Deidre asked, "What happened to the mother?"

"From the looks of it, she bled to death, poor thing."

Deidre asked, "Do you know her?"

"I've never seen her before. Do you know her, Leann?"

"No, Mama."

Kathleen raced back to the barn with the items Ellen needed.

She said, "I didn't warm the milk."

"It can't be helped. We got to save this baby, because her mama died giving her life!"

Ellen and Kathleen worked quickly to get the baby cleaned and wrapped up. Ellen held the sweet little thing and prayed she would accept the milk.

"Come on baby girl, this is good milk."

Deidre smiled and said, "Well, I'll be. She's taking it."

"That's it baby girl. I knew you were hungry."

Finally, Leann got control of her emotions and commented, "She has such tiny feet and a head full of brown hair like her mama."

Deidre asked, "How did the mother git here?"

Ellen answered with tears on her cheeks, "From the looks of her shoes, she walked a long ways."

Leann added, "I didn't see a strange horse around."

Ellen fired back, "Honey child, you wouldn't have seen a herd of buffalo the way you were carrying on."

"I just got a little excited, Mama."

"You better change a little to hordes and hordes."

Kathleen mentioned, "I've never seen her around Fredericksburg, either."

Ellen went on, "With all the refuges leaving Yankee held territory, who knows where she came from."

Kathleen asked, "Do you think the baby is full term?"

"No, I'd say about eight months."

Ellen asked, "Leann, do you think you can get Harry's crib down from the loft without killing yourself?"

"For Pete's sake, Mama!"

Ellen continued, "Once you get it down without causing a major catastrophe, take it to the house and clean it up."

"For Pete's sake, Mama!"

"You said that already, sweet girl."

Leann climbed the ladder, found the crib, and took it to the house without causing an earthquake.

Kathleen grinned and said, "She's sleeping like an angel now that her tummy is full."

Ellen fired back, "I'm too old for all this excitement. Leann needs to stop scaring the bejesus out of me. Sometimes, that girl reminds me of a cave full of dumb bats flying around."

Deidre replied, "That's the truth. Maybe, she'll grow out of it."

Ellen responded, "She needs to speed up the growing."

Kathleen asked, "What are we going to name her?"

Ellen replied, "She looks like a southern belle, so let's call her Belle."

They all agreed Belle Elizabeth was perfect.

Before Deidre put an old blanket over the dead mother, she noticed she had a heart necklace on. She took it off and checked for an engraving, but there wasn't one. The poor mother didn't have a wedding ring on, either. A bundle next to the young woman only contained a few clothes and a blanket. There was nothing to identify who she was.

Kathleen asked, "Shouldn't we get the men folks?"

"Yes, because they need to take care of some things. Don't send Leann, because she'll be a hysterical wreck by the time she reaches them."

Deidre offered, "I'll get them."

Carefully, Kathleen and Ellen took the baby back to

the house and got her settled in the crib.

Grace smiled and said, "She's such a little, precious thing. You are right, Aunt Ellen, Belle is a perfect name."

Ellen sat back in her rocking chair and fanned herself.

She mentioned, "Between the Yankees and this, I've lost five years off my life."

Grace commented, "Can you imagine what Uncle Homer would do if we told him you had a baby in the barn?"

"Lord have mercy, child! He'd drop plum dead right here on the spot!"

They all giggled until their sides hurt. Ellen wasn't fooling anyone, because she always handled a crisis better than anybody else.

Ellen suggested, "Grace, make sure those men don't run straight through the front door. They must be calm and quiet, because we don't want to wake up Belle."

"Yes, ma'am! I'll keep them quiet."

Kathleen suggested, "I think the men should change her dirty diapers."

"Excellent idea! I guess we better fix her some tiny diapers."

Kathleen offered, "She can use Andy's baby clothes."

"That's good. I might have some material in my sewing box we can use. too."

When Deidre told her father-in-law and Uncle Homer about the baby, both men stood there frozen with their mouths wide open.

"For Pete's sake! Close your mouths and git to the house. There's things you need to do."

When the men folk got to the house, Grace told them

to be calm and quiet. If they didn't, Grace was going to take an iron skillet to their behinds.

The men folk walked into the house quietly and stood around the crib with eyes as big as tea cups.

Ellen whispered, "All of ya'll look like you just saw a monkey."

Homer knelt down by the crib and asked, "What is it?"

"It's a baby girl named Belle."

Arthur remarked, "Don't that beat all."

Ty mentioned, "I didn't know babies were that little. Harry was a big baby."

Harry added, "She's in my crib. I'm glad she fits in it."

Teddy smiled and asked, "Can we hold her?"

"Not yet, because she's too little."

Homer grinned like an opossum and said, "She's a cute little thing."

Ellen ordered, "You boys better be quiet around her."

"We will."

Teddy asked, "Can Belle be our secret?"

Arthur answered, "Yes! No one is to say anything about her mother, or how the baby got here. Do you understand?"

"Yes, sir."

Deidre spoke up and asked, "I'd love to take care of her. Can she sleep in my room?"

Ellen answered, "Alright, that will be a great help to me."

Homer, Arthur, and the boys got busy digging a grave and cleaning up the straw in the barn. The young mother was buried with the cavalrymen. Now, they had six unknown graves.

Faces of the Civil War

CHAPTER 11

On June 9th, Union Gen Benjamin Butler ordered 4,500 troops from his army to attack the outer most earthworks called the Dimmock Line. The trench line was defended by 2,500 men, teenage boys, and old men commanded by Confederate Gen Pierre Beauregard. Gen Butler was confident his forces could capture Petersburg, but because of poor leadership the assault failed. The Union let a golden opportunity slip away. Now, it would take a ten-month siege to capture Petersburg.

Gen Pierre Beauregard　　　　Gen Benjamin Butler

Gen Grant left Cold Harbor on June 12th and headed for Petersburg. Between the 15th and 18th of June, Confederate forces were stretched thinly along the ten mile long Dimmock Line from the Appomattox River and around the city.

Every Union assault failed to capture the city and its railroads. Poor leadership, unclear orders, and delays sabotaged Union plans to strike a deadly blow.

Gen A. P. Hill's III Corps was ordered to march 20 miles in the heat and humidity on June 18th to beat Gen Grant's army to Petersburg. The III Corps, including the
47th Virginia, crossed the James River and started digging trenches along the Appomattox River one mile from Petersburg. Gen Heth pushed his troops and got there just in time. The men were exhausted, hot, and foot sore, but they made it.

Gen Grant was furious with several general officers for their poor and timid leadership. He relieved one of his generals from command.

Gen Winfield Hancock, commanding general of the Union II Corps, fell ill from the lingering wounds he suffered at Gettysburg. Gen David Birney took over Hancock's command, but he wasn't Gen Hancock of Gettysburg.

Gen Grant was saddened to find out Col Joshua Chamberlain, Medal of Honor winner at Gettysburg, was severely wounded and wasn't expected to live. Grant issued Chamberlain a battlefield promotion to brigadier general. If all his colonels and generals were like Chamberlain, he could have ended the war in June.

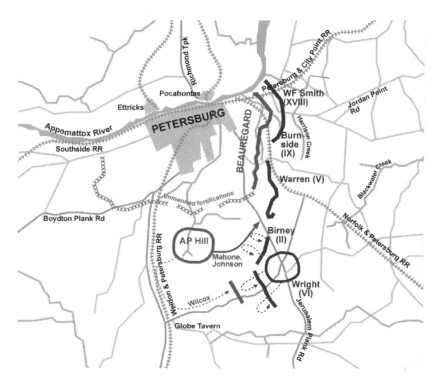

On June 18th around noon, Gen Meade ordered an assault on the Dimmock trenches. Now, he had the IX and the V Corps to join the fight. Part of the IX Corps got bogged down in the marshy terrain and open areas around Taylor's Branch and suffered heavy casualties.

The V Corps didn't fare any better. Gen Warren's corps ran into a wall of artillery and musket fire that stopped Gen Warren where the Jerusalem Plank Road(Rt. 301) met the Dimmock Line

Gen David Birney   Gen Gouverneur Warren

At 6:30 pm, Gen Meade ordered another attack against the entrenched Confederates. The 1st Maine Heavy Artillery Regiment had spent most of the war guarding Washington, D. C. Now, these 900 men were infantrymen in one of the leading regiments. The assault was met with horrendous fire and failed. The regiment suffered 632 casualties. No regiment in the Union army suffered that many casualties in one day.

During the four days of attacks, the Union lost over 11,000 men compared to Confederate losses set at around 4,000 men.

The 47th Virginia spent June 19th and June 20th digging and fortifying trenches. The Confederate soldiers manning the Dimmock Line were busy building shelters, so they could get out of the hot sun and rain. Just when they had their trenches all set up, Gen Fry's brigade was ordered to Fort Clifton where Swift Creek merged into the Appomattox River.

While at Fort Clifton, the brigade was assigned picket

duty. Gen Fry became ill, so command of the brigade went back to Col Mayo. The men figured since the brigade was short on officers Col Mayo was better than none. Command of the 47th Virginia went to LtCol John Lyell, again.

Clay complained, "I hate moving all over the place. We git our trenches and fortifications just right, then we have to move into somebody else's trenches. Some aren't as good as others.

Gus continued, "We're at Fort Clifton until July 4th. Then, we have to march back to Petersburg. If we didn't do so much marching, we wouldn't wear out our shoes, socks, and feet."

Aaron teased, "Make sure you tell Gen Lee about the problem."

David joined in, "Don't forget marching eight miles to Ream's Station on July 10th. Then, it's march back to Petersburg."

Pvt James Watson added, "I'm sure my feet are going to fall off before the war is over."

Micah went on, "Ain't that the truth! I say we collect all our lice and chiggers and let them whip on the Yankees."

Clay fired back, "You can have all my varmints. Don't forget to add the dog flies and mosquitoes."

Pvt Douglas mentioned, "I'd pay money to watch swarms and swarms of our insects attacking the Union army wherever they are!"

Pvt Musselman commented, "That would sure be a sight to see. Can't you picture the Yankees jumping into the James and Appomattox Rivers?"

All the men laughed until they ran out of energy. At least, the men could still laugh.

During this span of time, the men in the brigade were told about a raid carried out by Union soldiers and marines in the counties on the Northern Neck. They stole livestock, and hundreds of slaves were freed. Mills were burned, farm equipment was destroyed, and empty buildings were looted and burned.

The men were furious, but weren't surprised after watching what happened in Fredericksburg. They worried about their families, because letters from home were barely getting to the soldiers. The men felt so useless, because they couldn't go home to help fight raids like this one.

Micah fumed, "My parents lost their home in Fredericksburg and moved in with my aunt and uncle in Lancaster. The Yankees probably stole their livestock and destroyed their farm equipment. Why did they destroy things my folks need to grow food? That ain't right! They could starve to death!"

David mentioned, "Abner's folks moved between Bowling Green and Tappahannock. I pray they weren't affected."

Aaron commented, "The captain didn't say anything about raiding in Caroline County."

Clay went on, "The Yankees are doing the same thing in the Shenandoah Valley."

Gus fussed, "Sherman is doing the same thing in the western theater. They're trying to starve our army to death. They don't care about how many civilians they starve while they're at it."

Micah fumed, "The sutlers are no better. They keep raising prices on everything, so the average person can't afford it. Shoot fire! None of us have enough money to buy anything!"

Clay added, "I heard a rumor about storekeepers in

Richmond raising prices so high only the rich people can afford to buy supplies and food. That ain't right, either. I wonder how many folks are starving to death, because of those greedy devils."

David mentioned, "Somehow, we have to win the war to put an end to this madness. Our state is being destroyed inch by inch, and our people are being starved to death."

Mayo's brigade received marching orders on July 27th, because the Yankees were attacking the Confederate line north of the James River. Quickly, the men marched through Petersburg and boarded a train that took them near Drewry's Bluff. After getting off the train, the brigade crossed the James River.

Gus asked, "Where the crap are we going?"

Cpl Steptoe Washington answered, "Deep Bottom. It's near a horseshoe-shaped bend in the James River called Jones Neck."

Aaron fumed, "Well, I'd like to break Jones's neck right about now! I'm going to be really mad if this Deep Bottom is a swamp, Cpl Bigtoe!"

Cpl Steptoe laughed and continued, "We're ordered to occupy trenches under the command of Gen Richard Anderson."

Gen Grant's plan was to have Gen Hancock's II Corps attack Deep Bottom, Chaffin's Bluff, and then pin down the Confederate forces while Gen Sheridan's cavalry attacked the Virginia Central Railroad. Grant was counting on Gen Lee pulling forces away from Petersburg to re-enforce troops fighting these attacks near Richmond.

Gen Grant wanted Confederate forces pulled away from Petersburg, because a tunnel had been dug under a section of the Confederate lines in Petersburg. It was packed full of explosives under the Rebel line and ready to be set off. The date for this action was set for July 30th.

The Union forces kept Confederate troops busy at Bailey's Creek, Fussell's Mill, New Market Road, New Market Heights, and Long Bridge Road.

Mayo's brigade, including the 47th Virginia, was involved in some skirmishes and subjected to some artillery fire.

At the First Battle of Deep Bottom, the Union losses were almost 500 men. Confederate losses were around 700 men.

DEEP BOTTOM

On July 30th north of Baxter Road, the explosives at the end of the tunnel under Elliott's Salient exploded creating an enormous hole in the trench line. Debris and bodies were thrown in every direction. Over 250 Confederate soldiers from South Carolina regiments were killed, instantly.

Three Union divisions attacked, but instead of going around the giant crater many soldiers ended up in it. The crater would be a death trap for many soldiers in blue. Union casualties would be over 4,000 men. The Union soldiers were unable to breech the line and roll up each side.

Col Mayo's brigade was sent to relieve Colquitt's brigade to the right of the crater on August 1st. In front of the 47th Virginia were the Union trenches only 200 yards away.

David looked around and said, "My God, what have we done to each other?"

Aaron added, "I can hear buttons popping and seams ripping open on the uniforms. It's just like Cold Harbor."

Clay remarked, "The hot sun has baked the dead black just like at Cold Harbor."

Poor Micah had the dry heaves from the stench like he did at Cold Harbor.

Cpl Steptoe told the men a truce had been arranged to recover any wounded and bury the dead.

Pvt Elijah Patterson commented, "Maybe, the Yanks can save more men than they did at Cold Harbor."

The brigade crawled out of their trenches and started digging long trenches to bury the dead.

Both sides spent about six hours in the blazing, hot sun completing the gruesome task. The two sides talked to each other like there was no war going on. Afterwards, they traded coffee, tobacco, newspapers, and a few other items. Of course, the Confederates took anything they needed from the dead. The Yanks didn't stop the Rebels from taking what they needed.

David, Gus, and Clay got shoes and socks. Aaron found drawers, a shirt, comb, and Yankee money. Micah got shoes, socks, drawers, and Yankee money. The boys figured the Yanks must have gotten paid.

Cpl Steptoe and some of the others carried several knapsacks back to their trenches. When the time was up, the boys crawled back into their trench line and shared the booty Cpl Steptoe was handing out. Finally, the men could eat something and not still be hungry.

Life in the trenches was dreadful, because of the heat, humidity, constant sniping, skirmishing, artillery fire, and the swarms of dog flies and insects. When it was dry, the wind blew the red clay everywhere. It produced a red dust cloud that coated everything. The dust got into the soldier's eyes, mouth, nose, and hair. If it rained the bottom of the trenches turned into a quagmire of mud. All the trenches were unsanitary and unhealthy.

The 47th Virginia learned how to deal with mortar fire for the first time. The men dreaded the mortar shells more than the artillery shells. All the men prayed another tunnel wouldn't explode under them. Because of this, Gen Heth ordered his division under arms at 2:00 am, in case, there was another explosion.

The men couldn't crawl out of their trenches and answer the call of nature. A sharpshooter fired at anything that moved on each side. Trench warfare and sharpshooters meant a soldier couldn't pee in the bushes anymore.

Finally, on August 13th, Col Mayo's brigade was relieved and sent to the rear to rest and recover from their ordeal in the trenches. The men were so glad to sleep in a tent in the open and be above ground. What they wanted most was a bath and sleep.

During this period, the 47th Virginia lost Pvt John Terry from Co. K who was mortally wounded. Drummer William Rosson from Co. K was wounded in the left leg which required amputation.

Faces of the Civil War

CHAPTER 12

Homer called the family together after dinner and told them about the Union raid on the Northern Neck. One could hear a pin drop for several seconds.

Harry asked, "Are they coming here, Poppa?"

"I don't know, but we must be prepared just the same."

Teddy asked, "Did they kill people, Uncle Homer?"

"Not that I know of, but we must be prepared for anything. We have to protect Andy and little Belle."

Ty commented, "We won't let you down, Poppa. We all love each other."

Arthur remarked, "No one goes anywhere alone on the farm. All of you women know how to protect yourselves and use a weapon. Keep your weapons close by, but remember about Andy. We don't want him getting his hands on one."

Homer ordered, "Keep a good lookout all the time. Leann, you can't fall to pieces and turn into a babbling crier."

"Don't worry, Poppa, I'll keep a calm head."

Ellen suggested, "If you don't, girl, someone could get killed."

"I promise you, I'll be strong."

Homer continued, "The area we cleared back in the woods a couple of years ago will still be used for extra supplies and food, but no livestock. I don't want anybody going back and forth feeding the animals. Arthur and I believe it's too dangerous."

Ellen suggested, "Let's bring lots more firewood close to the house and several buckets of water. That will cut down on the trips to the well."

"That's a good idea. You boys git on that as soon as we're finished here."

"Yes, sir!"

Arthur mentioned, "Use your common sense to think things through. Remember, stupid people make stupid mistakes. Desperate people will do just about anything to get what they want. Foolish folks make mistakes. Don't be stupid or foolish."

Ellen added, "If we work together and stay alert, we should be fine."

Grace smiled and said, "Aunt Ellen, I wouldn't lock horns with you for nothin' in this here world."

"You are a very smart girl."

Homer asked, "Are there any questions?"

Teddy asked, "Can I still go fishing?"

"Not by yourself, but let's hold off on that, right now."

Arthur went on, "From now on, we'll lock the front door at night. The back door stays locked all the time."

"Also, no outhouse at night, you'll have to use a bucket. We don't want anyone jumped outside at night."

"Yes, sir!"

Homer ordered, "Alright boys, git busy on the water buckets and firewood."

"Yes, sir!"

Once the boys were gone, Homer commented, "We have nine hours that need to be covered on night watch. I'll take three hours, Arthur takes three, and someone else needs to cover three hours."

Grace spoke up and said, "I'll take three."

"Alright, that's settled."

Leann suggested, "I can relieve Uncle Arthur and Poppa some of the time."

"Alright, but remember no hysterical outbursts, young lady!"

"I promise, Poppa."

Homer and Arthur stepped outside on the porch and looked around.

Arthur admitted, "I never thought any of this could happen. I was living in a nice home with a good profession. Then, my dear wife was taken from me, and my sons marched off to war. I have no idea where they are. Since the Wilderness, I don't know if they're still alive. Now, war is on our doorstep."

Homer responded, "I know how you feel. I'm asking myself if I can keep my family safe along with little Belle. Sometimes, I feel very alone. Our sons already know about the horrors of war. How do they cope with it every day?"

"I don't know. The only thing we can do is pray we'll do the right thing and our best. He'll watch over us. What I want to see most of all is our boys walking up your wagon road with outstretched arms."

Homer went on, "Then, Virginia will face the monumental task of recovering and healing. All of us will have to pick up the pieces of our lives and put them back together, again."

Arthur asked, "Will we have the pieces to pick up?"

"That's the mystery, my brother."

Arthur continued, "I pray Grace and Teddy will remain strong and dependable."

"I pray for the same thing from Ty, Harry, and Leann."

Arthur laughed and remarked, "Leann can go off the deep end on occasion, but I think she'll do fine."

Homer chuckled, "That daughter of mine can sure get feisty, at times."

Over the next several days, the family kept a sharp lookout as they went about their chores. The night watches were going smoothly.

Homer's closest neighbor stopped by to let them know the raid on the Northern Neck was over, but it left many folks terrified. He told them about the Battle of the Crater, and they wondered if their sons were alright. The last letters the Murphy family received from the boys were from before Christmas.

Once Gen Grant kept moving southward, the Yankees were taking over more and more territory, and mail wasn't getting through. The Murphy families realized their sons probably didn't have ink and paper to write a letter. So many items were getting hard to find. Also, the Murphy families realized Lincoln's blockade and total warfare policy were taking a toll on the southern states. They hoped Lincoln would lose the presidential election, and the North would stop fighting the Confederacy.

One hot, humid day in August, Grace and Leann went to the barn to get more feed for the chickens. The men had left about fifteen minutes ago to work in the fields. Suddenly, both girls were grabbed from behind, a hand covered their mouths, and a pistol put to their heads.

One deserter ordered, "If either one of you fights or makes a sound, we're going to pull the trigger!"

Of course, both girl's minds were racing to figure out how to get out of this terrible situation. Grace hoped Leann wouldn't do anything stupid and get both of them killed.

Leann thought, "I can't go crazy. Be calm! Think this problem through. Grace and I have to stop these two deserters before they go to the house."

Leann's deserter said, "I ain't had no woman in over two years. Mine smells real good and feels soft as a kitten. How about your gal, Marvin?"

He replied, "Oh, she be mighty soft and right smart pretty."

"Don't you be a wantin' a woman, Marvin?"

"Sure thing! We can take whats we want. The horses can wait 'til we has a real big treat!"

Grace thought, "Sweet Jesus, they are lusting after us!"

Leann thought, "So, you varmints want loving. Well, I have a surprise waiting for you."

The deserter turned Leann around and ordered, "Take them clothes off, missy!"

Leann blabbed, "I ain't had no man in a long time. You look mighty goods to me. Let's get naked as jay birds and has lots of fun in this fresh straw."

Grace thought, "Lord Almighty, what are you thinking about, Leann? Have you gone raving crazy? We're plum dead, now, because you went off the deep end."

Grace's deserter whirled her around, grinned, and ordered, "Times a wastin', gal! Git them there clothes off!"

Leann blabbed, "Come on, Grace. You wants a man as bad as I do. These fellers need some good ole southern belle lovin'. It's our duty to help our poor soldiers with anything they be a needin' and wantin'."

"That's right, missy!"

Grace thought, "I'm going to die, because you're stupid! If I wasn't about to die, I'd kill you plum dead myself, Leann!"

Leann giggled, "Let's get these here clothes off and git down to business. These brave boys haven't had lovin' in a long time."

Teddy stayed hidden and listened to what Leann was saying. She was up to something. He wasn't going to let anything happen to his sister and cousin. He'd be ready if one of those dirty varmints put their hands on the girls. He had the element of surprise on his side. Those varmints had no idea he was in the barn when they came inside.

As if in slow motion, Leann's soldier put his revolver in his holster, dropped his holster and pants, and was unbuttoning his jacket just like the other deserter.

Leann hit her deserter with a swift kick in between his legs, and he dropped to the floor in agony. Leann grabbed a shovel close by and slammed it down on the deserter's head crushing his skull.

Teddy thinks, "Steady! I got to do this right. Aim. Take the shot!"

As soon as Grace realized what was happening, her deserter fell to his knees with an arrow through his neck spraying blood on her.

Teddy ran up to the girls and said, "Leann, you were great! I was ready to kill them varmints, but I knew you were up to something!"

Leann asked, "Why are you in the barn?"

"Uncle Homer needed a hammer and nails."

Leann asked Grace, "Are you alright?"

Grace was shaking and blabbed, "You scared the living bejesus out of me! I thought you were plum crazy, and both of us were going to die! You have more grit than I do! I would never have thought about kicking them in the privates. You and Teddy saved us!"

Ellen was getting lunch started when she saw the back door knob move. Quickly, she grabbed her revolver and made sure little Andy was inside. The knob moved some more, so Ellen took aim and fired two shots plum through the door.

Teddy took off for the house with his bow and arrows, Grace grabbed a pitchfork, and Leann grabbed the shovel. Teddy saw one deserter stumble off the back porch holding his stomach while another one started running.

Teddy thinks, "You're not going to hurt our family. Aim. Take your shot!"

Grace slammed her pitchfork into the deserter Teddy had shot. Ellen came flying around the corner of the house just as Leann smashed her shovel on the other varmint's head.

Teddy shouted, "It's alright, Aunt Ellen! We took care of the two deserters. There's two more varmints in the barn dead."

Ellen asked, "What happened in the barn? You're bleeding, Grace!"

Grace blabbed, "It's not mine. Those dirty varmints wanted to lust on us! Leann was real brave and kicked one of them in his privates! Teddy took care of the other deserter!"

Ellen's mouth dropped wide open, but she couldn't seem to talk.

Teddy shouted, "Aunt Ellen, you were real brave shooting that deserter plum through the back door!"

All Ellen could do was gather Teddy, Grace, and Leann in her arms. Poor Grace and Leann burst into tears, but they alright. Now, they could fall apart!

Meanwhile in the fields, the men heard two shots, grabbed their guns, and raced to the house. Arthur and Ty slowly went into the barn. They saw the two dead deserters.

Ty asked, "Why do they have their pants down and their behinds showing?"

Arthur answered, "They didn't get what they wanted from the girls."

Ty responded, "Oh, I get it, now. Those filthy monsters!"

Homer and Harry raced to the backyard and stopped dead in their tracks dumbfounded.

Ellen blabbed, "All of us know the back door is locked. Someone was up to no good. I figured I'd shoot and ask questions, later. By the way, I'm getting too old for this manure. This is too much excitement for one day."

Teddy and Grace jumped into their father's arms, and Homer hugged Ellen and Leann.

Kathleen and Deidre came out with their weapons ready for anything. When they heard the story, neither one of them could believe Leann talked the guns right out of those deserter's hands.

Harry asked, "Leann, did you really smash that varmint's head and cut off his ear?"

"Yes, I did! I accidently cut his ear off."

Harry asked, "Grace, did you stab that deserter with a pitchfork?"

I sure did! We had to do something to protect Andy and Belle."

Harry mentioned, "I don't ever want you two girls mad at me!"

"Hush up, Harry," Leann teased.

Ty came up and teased, "That's right! They'll make us plum dead in a hurry!"

Arthur looked around and commented, "I can't believe my eyes! That was some quick thinking. I'm proud of all of you."

Kathleen said, "You'll always be my heroes!"

Deidre added, "You sure whipped up on that bunch of scum!"

Grace fired back, "Those varmints should have stayed in the army!"

Homer laughed and said, "With you four on duty, the rest of us don't need to be worried."

At that point, the group burst out laughing to help relieve the tension. What a crazy day, but they were all safe and no one got hurt.

The men buried the deserters back with the other dead. Homer didn't say any words from the Good Book.

Leann remarked, "You can have fun with some women in hades!"

Everyone knew Leann had entered a new phase in her life. She was a woman to be respected, now.

Arthur patted Homer on the back and said, "I guess we better build a new door."

Ellen blabbed, "You do that, because we did all the dirty work including a very brave, Teddy."

Homer fired back, "Amen. brothers and sisters!"

CHAPTER 13

In August 1864, Gen Grant was determined to cut the railroads converging in Petersburg. The Union army had to capture these railroads and cut off the supplies getting to Gen Lee's army. The Weldon Railroad carried supplies from North Carolina. Many of these supplies were coming from the only seaport the Confederacy still controlled.

Gen Grant chose Gen Gouverneur Warren's V Corps, some elements from the IX Corps, the II Corps, and a division of cavalry to gain control of the Weldon Railroad.

On August 18th, Gen Warren's men marched in the soaking rain over muddy roads to Globe Tavern around 9:00 am. Union troops tore up tracks until around 1:00 pm. Gen Warren sent Union troops northward along the tracks in case the Confederates decided to attack them.

Globe Tavern

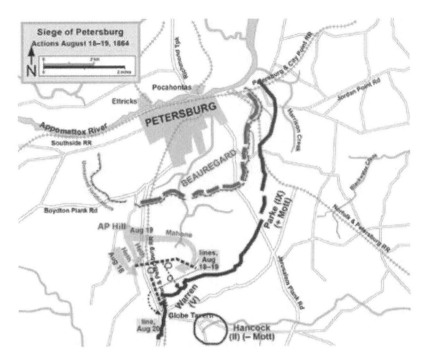

Gen A. P. Hill ordered some of Gen Heth's brigades to march southward and
re-capture the railroad. Gen Heth put Col Mayo's brigade on the left side of the tracks and Gen Davis's brigade on the right side. They were ordered to attack.

The soldiers in Col Mayo's brigade knew the Yankees were after the railroads. They had to run the Yankees away, because the Weldon Railroad was vital.

As the brigade and the 47th Virginia marched southward, they marched through a wooded area.

Aaron asked, "Where are the Yankees, Cpl Steptoe?"

He answered, "You can bet they're in the trees waiting for us. We have to move quickly to cross the fence and the open field. If we don't, we'll be cut to pieces."

The Union troops opened fire when the boys were

crossing the fence.

David yelled, "Hurry up, Aaron!"

Clay cussed, because he tripped going over the fence.

Gus's heart pounded when he crossed the fence. The order to charge raced through the ranks as the 47th Virginia sprinted for the tree line, firing as they advanced.

Micah thought, "I got to git to the trees! Are the Yanks well-fortified? We have to keep control of the railroad."

The 47th Virginia plowed into the tree line with their 178 officers and men. The entire regiment was down to the size of less than two companies.

Parts of the Union line were collapsing. Bloody hand-to-hand combat broke out as the Confederate troops kept driving the Union line down the railroad tracks.

Clay aimed and fired at a soldier running to the rear. He dropped to the ground. David thrust his bayonet into a Yank running at him with a knife. Gus jumped a Yank from behind and stuck his knife into his back. Micah grabbed a young Yank, but couldn't use his knife against him, so he knocked him out cold with his fist. He was only a young teenager.

Aaron aimed at a Yank, saw he was nothing but a kid, and fired at the soldier next to him. The young Yank threw down his gun and raised his arms to surrender. Aaron grabbed the youth and the kid burst into tears.

He begged, "Please, don't kill me! I surrender! Please, don't hurt me!"

Aaron asked, "How old are you?"

"I'm sixteen, sir! Don't kill me!"

Aaron took the youth to the provost guard and hurried to rejoin his friends.

The Union troops kept retreating suffering heavy losses as they withdrew.

Gen Warren sent in reinforcements to stop the wholesale retreat, and they were able to stabilize their lines.

David yelled, "The Yankees are hitting our flank! We're taking fire from two sides!"

An officer ordered the Confederates to form a line at the edge of the woods. Gen Warren's men plowed into Col Mayo's brigade around 6:00 pm.

Clay yelled, "Get behind this dead tree trunk! Pile anything we can in front of us!"

Micah shouted, "Bullets are flying everywhere! Branches and leaves are falling like snow!"

A bullet whacked the tree next to Gus, and he thought, "Sweet Jesus, that was too close!"

Aaron was hot and thirsty. His face and hands were black from gunpowder.

David saw a dead deer close to him, but he couldn't think about food, now.

The brigade fired volley after volley into the Union ranks holding their line as darkness fell. Around 9:00 pm, Gen Heth pulled his brigades out of the woods and marched them back to their Petersburg trenches.

While marching back to their lines, Gus asked, "Why are we leaving our position in the woods?"

Aaron fired back, "Don't these generals know they're giving that position back to the Yankees?"

Pvt Charlie Jones shot back, "It seems mighty stupid to me. We fought all confounded day in them woods!"

Pvt John Stewart commented, "Don't make a lick of sense to me. Of course, lots of things don't make sense in the army."

David replied, "Amen, brothers and sisters!"

Micah asked, "Are you sure a lot of our generals ain't chiggers?"

Gus slapped Micah's shoulder and said, "Next time you see Gen Lee ask him if he's a chigger."

Micah fired back, "I ain't talking about Gen Lee!"

Clay chimed in, "In my valuable opinion, lots of officers are chiggers, because they are a pain in the behind."

The boys had a good laughing session that helped ease the frustration and tension.

During the night, Union troops entrenched and received reinforcements. Gen Heth was sent a cavalry division and three brigades from Gen William Mahone.

On August 19th around 4:00 pm, Gen Heth marched his men in a pouring rainstorm to attack the Union entrenched lines. As the men were marching through thick underbrush, they noticed whortleberries and helped themselves.

One soldier asked, "What are they?"

Gus answered, "They're some kind of blueberry. Eat up, because they are real tasty."

Not far from the Union lines, Gen Heth positioned the brigades and gave the order to charge. The Rebel brigades captured the first entrenchment and overran the second line. Union reinforcements kept arriving on the field, and Gen Heth's attack was in jeopardy.

One of Gen Mahone's brigades got too far out in front of the attack and almost got themselves surrounded. They managed to break free and get back to their lines.

David saw William Payne shot in the right arm while carrying the 47th Virginia battle flag. The brigade was ordered to fall back, because Union reinforcements were overwhelming their position. The 47th Virginia was making their way through the woods, and David lost sight of the regimental flag.

He yelled, "Where's the flag and color bearers?"

Aaron answered, "I don't see them."

Sgt Charles Brown from the 50th Pennsylvania Infantry saw Payne and the color guards picking their way through the trees. He took off after them, ordered them to surrender, and marched them back to the breastworks. Brown took the flag as Payne and the color bearers wept, because they had lost their regiment's flag. Every regiment's flag was considered sacred to its men. To the remaining men of the 47th Virginia, this was a bitter loss.

Sgt Charles Brown was awarded the Medal of Honor for capturing the flag and the color guard.

Gen William Mahone

Gen Heth sent Mahone's men back to their Petersburg line. Col Mayo's and Gen Davis's brigades stayed in their positions that night and the next two days in the pouring rain.

When it stopped raining on the morning of August 21st, Mahone's brigades attacked the Union left, and Gen Heth's brigades attacked the center. The attacks failed, so the Confederate brigades withdrew around 10:30 am. This was the Union's first victory during the siege of Petersburg, Now, the Confederates lost several valuable miles of the Weldon Railroad and would have to carry supplies by wagon 30 miles from the rail station at Stony Creek, northward on the Boydton Plank Road, and into Petersburg.

The Battle of Globe Tavern cost the Union over 4,000 casualties and cost the Confederacy over 1,600 men.

The 47th Virginia would suffer 15 casualties. Pvt J. T. Snelson from Co. H was killed in action, and the regiment's commanding officer, LtCol John Lyell was severely wounded in the left arm requiring amputation.

Col Mayo became ill, so command of the brigade went to Gen James Archer who was captured at Gettysburg and later exchanged. The 47th Virginia came under the command of Capt Edmund Wharton.

Harry was in the barn when he noticed Pepper and went over to love her. When he put his hand on her, he knew she was dead. He started to sob, gathered her up in his arms, and rocked back and forth weeping. He got up and walked towards the house holding his beloved pet, gently. The tears wouldn't stop running down his cheeks.

Harry whispered, "You were my friend, and you always loved me back. Why did you die alone? It just isn't fair, because there is too much dying going on. Why won't it stop? Why did you have to die?"

Ellen saw her youngest son coming towards the house with Pepper.

She thought, "Did she have a splinter in her paw, again?"

She walked out on the porch to see what was the matter. Suddenly, Harry rushed into her arms sobbing trying to tell her about his beloved cat.

She thought, "Sweet Jesus, the cat must be dead. Harry had a tender heart and a gentle soul much like Arthur's son, Teddy. However, when Harry got mad, look out, because fur was going to fly."

Between sobs, Harry said, "She's dead, Mama! It ain't right!"

Ellen consoled, "Pepper is in heaven with grandpa and grandma. It was her turn to go."

"Will they take care of her for me?"

"Of course, she'll get lots of loving from them."

"I want to bury her in a special place."

"Alright, you find a special place, and I'll wrap her up real pretty like."

Harry decided to bury her by the apple tree, because she always watched him pick apples. He dug a deep hole and went back to get her. His mother had wrapped her up real nice. Ellen went with Harry to the little grave. He covered her up and looked at his mama.

"It's your duty to say words over her grave like your poppa does."

Harry took a deep breath and said, "You were my

best friend ever. I loved you a whole lot. I knew you loved me, because you purred when I touched you. Say hello to grandpa and grandma for me. You can be their best friend, now. Was that alright, Mama?"

"That was mighty fine, son."

A couple days later at breakfast, Ellen commented, "My bones are telling me bad weather is coming. I don't mean a thunderstorm blowing through. It's going to be a real dust up, because I feel like a train hit me."

Homer added, "I guess that means we better start getting prepared before it blows in."

Teddy remarked, "Aunt Ellen, you felt that way when that snowstorm came through."

"That's right! I always listen to my bones."

Grace asked, "How much time do we have to get ready?"

"I'd say a day or two."

Homer went on, "Ty and I will run his trap lines and do some hunting. Harry, you move lots of firewood to the porch and put plenty in the house. Teddy fill up several buckets of water and fill the bathtub on the back porch."

Ellen ordered, "Leann, I want you to move extra feed to the chicken house and make sure everything is secure."

Arthur spoke up, "Grace and I will go to the fields and bring in lots of vegetables."

Kathleen continued, "Andy and I will pick the garden. He loves picking tomatoes, green beans, and squash."

Ellen suggested, "Harry, when you finish with the firewood, take Aunt Deidre to help you pick apples."

Leann chimed in, "Poppa, don't forget to fix the hinge on the barn door!"

"I won't."

The farm was a flurry of activity getting ready for the coming storm. No one complained, because they all knew what bad storms could do, so they had to be ready for anything.

Arthur and Grace brought back a wagon full of produce and headed out with the other wagon. Afterwards, they'd make sure feed for the cows and horses was close by.

Kathleen and Andy were having fun in the garden. Believe or not, Andy was a big help filling up the baskets. Of course, Kathleen let the little fellow eat a tomato even though some of it ended up on his shirt and shorts.

Homer and Ty came back with a bounty from the trap lines, plus two wild turkeys. Tomorrow, they hoped to have time to fish a little.

Harry and Deidre brought back two baskets of apples to add to the stores. Afterwards, Harry helped his mother store the produce in Ellen's cellar under the house which stayed cool year round.

Grace and Arthur were brushing down the horses when Grace asked, "Did you hear that, Poppa?"

Arthur got his gun and asked, "Hear what?"

"The noise coming from over there in the corner."

"No, I didn't hear it. Wait here while I check it out."

Grace grabbed a pitchfork and nodded. The last thing she wanted to see was another deserter or a Yankee.

Slowly, Arthur edged closer to the corner, and he heard the noise, too. The last thing he wanted to do was blast a hole in the barn, terrify the livestock, and ask questions, later like Ellen.

He edged closer thinking it might be a black snake or

rat.

He looked and said, "Well, I'll be! Come over here, Grace, and look at this."

She looked and said, "Shoot fire! I didn't know Puffy was pregnant! She sure picked the wrong time to have kittens."

"I think it's just the right time. Think Grace!"

Grace blabbed, "Oh Poppa, you're right! I know Harry will love them. They'll help heal his sad heart."

"Things happen for a reason, my dear Grace."

"It looks like Puffy only had two kittens, Poppa."

Both looked around, but they couldn't find any more little kittens. Arthur got a box, put some old cloths in it, and put straw on top.

He said, "That should protect mother and babies better, especially, with a storm coming."

Grace beamed with excitement, "I'll get Harry, but I won't tell him what the surprise is!"

Shortly, Grace came back with Harry and pointed him in the right direction. When he saw the box, his face turned bright as the sun. He dropped to the floor trying to hold back the tears. He stroked the two kittens with his gentle fingers and smiled. Now, his tears were from joy.

He said, "Puffy, your two babies are gray and white like you. They are real cute. I'll take real good care of them. I promise! I got lots of love to give them."

Grace suggested, "You do that, Harry."

Arthur added, "The one with more white is a boy, and he has a sister."

"What are you going to name them?"

"I got to think a spell on it."

Grace asked, "Do you think your mama will let you keep them inside during the storm?"

"She has to! They could drown, git washed away, or starve to death!"

Arthur couldn't help but laugh. That boy could sure get dramatic like Leann when he wanted to.

"I tell you what, Harry. Let's all take Puffy and her babies in the house. It will be hard for your mama to say no to all three of us. Always remember, there's power in numbers. Harry, you turn on the tears, and I'll turn on the bull."

Harry jumped into his uncle's arms and gave him a big bear hug.

The threesome headed for the house with their precious nursery. When they got inside, Ellen saw the box and assumed there was produce in it.

She ordered, "Arthur, put the box in the cellar for right now."

"We found these in the barn and thought you might want them in the house."

She stomped over to Arthur and looked down. Her hands flew onto her hips, and Arthur could just about see fire coming out of her nose.

She blabbed, "Sweet Jesus, you know good and well cats stay in the barn!"

Harry went into action. He worked up some real big tears and said, "Please Mama, there's a bad storm coming, and they'll drown in the barn!"

Harry worked up a real good sobbing fit and said, "Please Mama, they have to be safe!"

Arthur responded, "I guess I could shoot them. That way they won't drown!"

Harry let out a big sob and grabbed Grace saying,

"Please, don't let Uncle Arthur murder my kittens! You got to stop him, Grace!"

"Your mama wants us to kill the kittens," Grace remarked with a straight face.

Ellen blabbed, "Now hold on a cotton picking minute! I didn't say anything about murder!"

Harry worked up another good sobbing fit with lots of tears.

He said, "Belle was born in the barn, and you let her sleep in the house."

Ellen fumed, "Harry Murphy, I ought to tan your hide. Belle is a person that Jesus sent us."

Harry worked up more tears and replied, "Jesus sent us these kittens to take care of."

Ellen fussed, "Lord deliver me! When I wake up in the morning, my hair is going to be snow white!"

Arthur asked, "Do you want me to shoot the kittens and Puffy?"

Harry fell to the floor sobbing.

He begged, "Please Uncle Arthur, don't murder my kittens!"

Ellen ordered, "Shut up, Arthur! Hush up, Harry!"

Arthur thought, "We sure do have you tied up in knots. One more round of tears from Harry should do the trick, quite nicely."

Just then, Homer came through the front door after fixing the barn hinge.

He asked, "What's all the commotion about?"

Arthur thought, "Go for it, Harry!"

The boy sobbed and rushed into his father's arms.

"What's the matter with you, son?"

"Mama wants Uncle Arthur to shoot the kittens dead! I have to take care of them, because Jesus sent them to me!"

"What kittens?"

Harry pulled his father over to the box and said, "These kittens. I want to love them!"

Arthur asked, "Do you want me to shoot the kittens, Homer?"

Ellen fussed, "Shut up, Arthur! The first time I smell cat pee and poop in this house the cats go back to the barn. Do you understand me, Harry?"

"Yes, Mama."

Arthur remarked, "It looks like I won't be shooting them unless they stink up the house."

"Arthur, I ought to take a frying pan to your head!"

While all this was going on, Ty, Leann, and Deidre were on the back porch trying not to bust a gut laughing. They knew Arthur and Grace were in on this charade. Homer wasn't doing too badly himself.

Harry asked, "Can I keep them in the bedroom?"

"I guess so. I'm going to the outhouse where I can get some peace and quiet. Don't any of you get me riled up. Homer, take your cotton picking brother outside and shoot him!"

"I'll get right on it!"

The group on the back porch got busy skinning rabbits and squirrels, because they didn't want Ellen to know they had a ring side seat to the big show.

Ellen stomped by them on her way to the outhouse in a mega fit, and nobody said a word. She slammed the outhouse door and sat down.

She started laughing in her apron and thought, "Boy, I sure got them riled up like a nest of rattlesnakes. There is nothing like some mental combat to get the blood flowing. My Harry sure is a rascal!"

Arthur mentioned, "I think that went quite well. By the way, Harry, you were great!"

Homer added, "I heard the circus going on in the house, so I waited a while before coming inside."

Grace asked, "Do you think Aunt Ellen is really mad at us?"

Homer laughed and replied, "No, honey. Your Aunt Ellen is like a peacock. She has to ruffle her feathers, at times. She's probably laughing right now and doesn't want us to know it."

Homer looked at Harry and Grace and suggested, "Make sure there's no pee or poop in the house."

"We will, sir."

After supper, Homer commented, "If we have a real gully washer, the wagon road will wash out like it did the last time. The creek that meanders through the woods will flood."

Harry spoke up, "That means we won't be able to fish."

"That's why we should go fishing in the early morning."

Ellen agreed, "That's a good idea! Just remember, when it starts to rain get your behinds back to the house in a hurry."

When Harry came out in the morning for breakfast, his mother gave him a small bowl of milk for Puffy.

Ellen suggested, "Put it on the porch, so she can drink and go take care of nature's call. She'll come back to feed her babies."

"Thanks, Mama."

Homer, Ty, Harry, and Teddy finished eating, quickly,

so they could get to the river and fish before the storm rolled in. Everybody took care of their chores hoping they'd be finished ahead of the brewing storm.

Arthur commented, "The humidity is thick enough to cut with a knife, and the clouds are building in the southeast."

Kathleen asked, "Aunt Ellen, how are your bones feeling, now?"

"They're giving me a fit! When my head starts hurting, the storm is close."

Deidre mentioned, "As soon as it starts raining, I'll take the tops off the water barrels."

"Thank you, dear. Belle is such a good baby, and she's growing from all the good milk and attention. I hope this storm doesn't scare her."

Arthur added, "I'm going to check all the shutters on the windows to make sure they're good and tight."

"Thank you, Arthur. You might make a farmer after all. By the way, I'm glad Homer didn't shoot you yesterday."

Arthur chuckled, because he was now back in Ellen's good graces.

Grace saw Puffy at the door, so she opened it.

She said, "Your babies are in the bedroom waiting for you."

Puffy sashayed her furry, little, southern belle behind back to the bedroom to feed her kittens.

Ellen remarked, "Just what I thought. She's taken over the house. Next thing you know, she'll throw our behinds out the door and make us sleep in the barn!"

Arthur jumped in, "I bet you'll win that fight!"

Ellen fired back, "Darn right I will!"

Grace chimed in, "Aunt Ellen, remember Puffy has

claws."

Ellen shot back, "And I, my dear, have a gun with real bullets. I play dirty!"

Everybody had a good laugh over the exchange, because they could just picture Ellen and Puffy in a shootout with bullets flying in every direction.

Homer and the boys caught a nice mess of fish, so they headed back to the house. They wanted to clean the fish before the heavens opened up.

All of them were starved, because fishing was hard work, in their opinion. They were looking forward to fried fish for supper.

Ellen and the girls were preparing lunch when Homer and the boys got back. The first thing Harry did was check on his kittens. Mother and babies were fast to sleep in their box.

Once the fish were cleaned, everybody sat down for lunch. While they were eating, they could hear thunder rolling in the distance. Homer looked outside and saw the black clouds in the southeast.

He mentioned, "I can tell you have a bad headache, honey."

"You are right, my dear husband."

Everybody finished eating, and the women told Ellen to sit down and rest her head. Ty took the tops off the rain barrels and closed the barn and chicken house doors.

The thunder was getting louder, and the clouds were almost black.

Teddy remarked, "Two deer just went racing across the yard. Too bad, I didn't have my bow and arrows to shoot them."

Homer responded, "They know Mother Nature is sending a storm this way."

Ty asked, "Does the army fight battles in storms like this?

Arthur answered, "I hope not. It would be hard to keep their powder dry. However, they fought at Spotsylvania Court House in the rain. I guess it depends on how bad the storm is."

The wind picked up with a fury, so Homer went around the house and closed the shutters. The women lighted more candles and waited.

A loud clap of thunder boomed, and the rain pounded the ground like hammers. Little Andy crawled up in his mother's lap, because loud thunder scared him. Deidre held Belle close, because she cried after that loud clap of thunder.

Homer and Arthur sat down at the table to play chess. Ty got his banjo out and started playing some tunes. Each person kept their mind occupied as the wind howled. Grace went around looking for any leaks in the house and went back to her knitting. All were thankful they had food to eat and a nice home to protect them. They knew their loved ones were suffering in trenches and in constant danger. They weren't safe from nature's wrath at any time.

Arthur stated, "We're having a lot of lightning with this storm."

Homer added, "I'm not surprised, because it's been so hot. Hopefully, it'll cool things down a bit."

Teddy went on, "I hope it'll kill all the mosquitoes."

Leann responded, "Maybe, it'll turn the mosquitoes into lightning bugs!"

Harry piped in, "Just think, we'll be able to see the mosquitoes when they land on us, and we can smash all their guts out."

Grace added, "Amen, brothers and sisters!"

Ellen commented, "Homer and Arthur, our children are a silly bunch, but we love them just the same."

Ty fired back, "Blame Teddy, he started it!"

Teddy shot back, "I hate mosquitoes!"

Ellen continued, "As far as I'm concerned, they're the scum of the earth right along with roaches!"

Arthur started laughing and said, "Checkmate, brother!"

Homer fired back, "You're cheating, but I can't catch you! You ain't that good of a chess player!"

"Face it Homer; you're a lousy chess player."

Another clap of thunder boomed and little Belle started crying, again. Deidre rocked and held her close while she talked to her in a soothing voice.

Ty got up to carry his banjo back to the bedroom, because he wanted to read a book for a while.

He looked at the bucket and thought, "There ain't no way I'm using this bucket until it's emptied."

He headed for the back porch, opened the door, and stepped out on the porch. He raced to the outhouse and dumped the bucket. As he was running back to the porch, he thought, "Shoot fire! I'm getting soaking wet."

Suddenly, there was a blinding flash of light followed by a cracking boom. Ty found himself flat on his face in the mud just short of the porch.

Homer jumped up and raced to the back porch with Arthur right behind him. Both men wondered why the

back door was open. They saw Ty face down in the
mud. Homer's heart jumped to his throat in panic.

He shouted, "Are you alright, son? What happened?"

Ty replied, "My back and nose hurt. I don't know
what happened!"

Arthur looked around and couldn't believe his eyes.
Everybody was crowded around the door, because that
flash scared the bejesus out of them, too!

Arthur announced, "The outhouse blew up in a
million pieces! Lightning must have hit it!"

Homer asked, "Ty were you in the outhouse?"

"No! I emptied our bucket, and then, I was in the
mud."

Ellen blabbed, "Sweet Jesus, you have to be alright!"

"I'm all wet and muddy! I hope I didn't get plastered
in poop!"

Ellen blabbed, "Lord have mercy, get that boy's
clothes off and wash him down."

They started taking his clothes off, carefully.

"Ouch Poppa, that hurts!"

Arthur said, "You have some splinters in your back.
We'll need to take them out, You were very lucky!
Thank the Lord, you weren't in the outhouse."

Leann got a pan, dipped it in the rain barrel, and gave
it to her father with a cloth. Homer washed Ty's face,
gently, and rinsed his hair.

The men got Ty's clothes off and rinsed him down the
best they could.

Arthur teased, "Ty, it looks like you survived the
exploding outhouse in pretty good shape!"

"I'm sure glad about that. Who wants to die in an
outhouse?"

Everybody laughed, because they knew Ty was very

fortunate to be alive.

Ellen ordered, "Harry get Ty a clean pair of pants and a nightshirt."

"Yes, ma'am. Don't worry Ty; we'll take real good care of you!"

Once Ty had clean pants on, the men helped him inside.

Grace spread a sheet over the table, so they could check him.

Kathleen started getting things her aunt would need to pull the splinters out of his back.

Ellen pulled them out and warned, "It's time for the vinegar, son. Try not to jump off the table and break your neck!"

"Do you have to use vinegar?"

"Son, you know it helps clean wounds."

"It always burns like fire!"

Harry blabbed, "You have to be brave, Ty. If you ain't, Leann will never let you forget it."

"Hush up, Harry," Leann fired back.

"Alright, Mama, let's get this over with."

Harry warned, "Leann, don't you say a word. Ty is going through some hurting. He could have been killed."

Of course, Ty wanted to cuss for at least ten minutes, but he knew better. His mama would swat his sore behind good. Right now, he didn't want any more pain. At this point, he already felt like a train just ran over him. Then, he felt ashamed, because his half-brothers and cousins were in constant danger and suffering in so many ways.

The storm lasted for three days, and Homer was

right. The wagon road was washed out, and the creek had flooded the area they went through to get to the river.

Everybody was glad to see the sunshine and get outdoors. Of course, the first order of business was building a new outhouse just a little bit bigger. Homer and Arthur had to check the buildings and crops for damage. The chicken house needed work done on the roof, but it wasn't serious. The barn made it through the storm with no damage. Homer hoped the fields weren't flooded, because they were planted on higher ground. Once Homer and Arthur checked them, they figured they lost about twenty per cent of their crops.

Ty and Harry checked the apple tree, saw some limbs blown down, and gathered the apples on the ground.

Leann spent quite a while talking to her chickens. She figured the storm scared them, too. They needed some sweet talking to get them back to normal.

Teddy and Grace checked the fenced in pasture and found three trees blown over the fence line. That meant the downed trees had to be moved before they could repair the fences.

Teddy commented, "This is going to take a lot of work to cut these trees up, but we'll get firewood out of it."

Grace remarked, "There are so many trees down in the woods. We can cut them up for firewood. Oh look, Teddy, it's a black bear cub. Isn't it cute!"

Teddy grabbed Grace's hand and started running towards the house.

"That cub's mama is close by, so we got to git out of here in a hurry! That mama will tear us up if she lights out after us!"

Grace's heart pounded as they ran as fast as they

could. Teddy slipped in the mud, but got up and willed his shaking legs to run.

Grace yelled, "Is she behind us?"

"I don't know!"

Then, they both heard the bear roar.

Teddy shouted, "Run faster, I can just see the house!"

Grace asked, "Where do we go?"

"Head for the chicken house and slam the door behind us!"

Kathleen was on the front porch when she saw Teddy and Grace running in panic towards the house.

She thought, "Don't tell me they saw a snake and are running like two fools."

She went into the house and told Ellen what was happening. Ellen grabbed her revolver and shotgun. Kathleen grabbed her revolver, as well. Both wondered why the two were headed towards the chicken house.

Ellen asked, "What are those two youngens up to?"

Kathleen shouted, "Sweet Jesus, a black bear is close behind them!"

Ellen ordered, "Git me more shotgun shells out of the hutch!"

Kathleen raced inside, grabbed a box, and rushed back to Ellen. Both women headed towards the chicken house, because they understood what the two kids had in mind. They must have run up on the bear or on her cub.

Teddy and Grace shot inside the chicken house, and Teddy slammed the door. By then, the mama bear was about 20 yards behind them. The two gasped for breath as sweat rolled down their faces. Their legs felt like tree trunks and burned like fire.

Ellen figured, "I'll fire off a blast close by hoping to scare the bear off. If that doesn't work, I'll fire both barrels even if it knocks me on my butt. Where are the men when you need them?"

Ellen fired one barrel to the right of the bear. It stopped, looked around, and just stood there. Ellen rammed another shell in the shotgun, and Kathleen had her revolver ready to shoot.

She asked, "Why isn't the bear moving?"

Ellen answered, "I guess its sizing us up. I'm firing one more shell to see if the darn thing will leave."

Ellen fired off another blast a little closer and this time the bear headed straight for Ellen and Kathleen.

Kathleen shouted, "I think you made it real mad!"

Ellen rammed another shell in the barrel, took aim........Pow! Pow! Pow! Pow! Pow!

The bear dropped about ten yards from Ellen and Kathleen. Ellen whirled around, and there stood five Yankee soldiers.

The lieutenant asked, "Please ladies, could you lower the shotgun and revolver before somebody gets hurt?"

Ellen demanded, "Who the hades are you?"

"Lieutenant Parker, ma'am. You aren't a very good shot, so we had to drop the bear before it had you for supper."

"I was trying to run it off, you idiot! I don't like killing unless it's necessary!"

One soldier said, "That bear's a mean one."

"How would you know, Yankee?"

"Because he attacked one of my men. I need your help, ma'am. My trooper is in bad shape."

"And just where is this trooper?"

"Back down the wagon road with the rest of my

company."

"Bring him up here and no Yankee tricks, or I'll let you have it with both barrels!"

Teddy and Grace stuck their heads out of the chicken house door and wondered what was happening. They heard all the shots and saw the dead bear. Teddy and Grace ran towards their Aunt Ellen and Kathleen.

Teddy yelled, "You better not hurt our Aunt Ellen, or I'll fight you to the death, Yankee!"

Lt Parker replied, "Don't worry, we won't."

Homer and Arthur heard the shots and raced back to the house, because they just knew Yankee cavalry had attacked their families.

Homer yelled, "If those murdering Yankees harm our families, I'll hunt them down if it takes me a year!"

Arthur added, "I'll be right beside you, brother."

When the two got within sight of the house, they stopped in their tracks.

Arthur asked, "What the hades is going on?"

"I don't know. Ellen would be blasting away if they were up to no good. There'd be dead Yankees all over the ground."

The two men took off running towards the house with guns ready and got there about the same time as the mauled trooper.

Ellen commented, "Hold on Homer, they need help. It's the least we can do since they killed the bear."

Teddy blabbed the whole story to his father.

Ellen went into her nurse mode after she looked over the trooper. Sure enough, he was in a bad way. Kathleen went inside and got the kitchen table set up for Ellen, so she could tend to the trooper. Grace was getting the items she would need including the dreaded vinegar.

She yelled, "It's all clear, Deidre!"

When Ty, Leann, Harry, and Deidre heard the gun shots, they barricaded themselves in Deidre's bedroom. Ty had a shotgun, Deidre a revolver, and Harry a knife ready to defend Little Belle and Andy to the death.

Carefully, the Union cavalrymen moved the trooper inside and sat him on the table.

Harry shouted, "Thems Yankees!"

"Hush up, Harry," Grace ordered.

Ellen ordered, "Git his jacket, shirt, trousers, and boots off, so I can see what needs to be done."

"Yes, ma'am."

"There's no doctor in these here parts, Lieutenant."

"Whatever, you can do to help my trooper, ma'am."

She asked, "How old are you, trooper?"

"I'm nineteen, ma'am."

Homer teased, "So, you're nineteen going on seventeen."

"Son, I'm going to have to sew up several of these claw wounds. It's going to hurt like the devil throwing a fit with his pitchfork! That ornery bear wanted you for a meal."

Homer spoke up, "I'll get a bottle of wine. Son, you drink all you need to cut the pain."

"Thank you, sir."

Harry commented, "My mama only has vinegar to help clean your wounds. You better drink the whole bottle of wine, because it'll burn like the devil threw you in the fireplace."

Ellen scolded, "Hush up, Harry!"

Harry changed the subject and said, "I really like your boots. When I git grown up, I'm going to git me a pair just like them."

"I like my booooots, toooo."

Homer noticed the trooper's face was getting red, and his tongue was getting mighty thick.

The trooper remarked, "It's hoot in hereee!"

Arthur suggested, "Drink up, boy. That's fine wine."

"I nevber haddd nooo wineee, afore."

Homer laughed and said, "This boy hasn't had any liquor before. He's feeling no pain!"

"Ma'am, I think my trooper is drunk already," the lieutenant said.

"That's a good thing. Alright young man, let's git you sewed up."

While Ellen sewed up the wounds, Leann gave the others some apple cider.

They said, "Thank you, ma'am, that tastes like heaven."

Arthur asked, "Why are you in this area?"

The lieutenant replied, "We're after some Union deserters that are a bad bunch. They killed two provost guards when they escaped. We tracked them to an abandoned cabin about two miles from here. They held up in the cabin during the storm. The bear jumped my trooper when we were checking the area around the cabin."

Homer asked, "How many are there?"

He responded, "Five."

Arthur asked, "Why are they headed south?"

"We think they might cut over to Port Royal to get into Maryland. Whatever they do, we'll catch them."

One of the others said, "The lieutenant will catch them, ma'am. They don't call him Hound Dog for nothing."

Harry chimed in, "That's a good nickname! My nickname is Hush Up, Harry!"

Leann warned, "You better behave, or Mama's going to tan your hide!"

Everyone broke out in laughter, because Harry could be hilarious.

Homer commented, "Your trooper won't be able to ride for a while. Besides, you don't want those cuts to git infected. You can leave him here, because we'll look after him. Then, you can come back for him, later."

Lt Parker responded, "That's mighty nice of you folks."

Arthur added, "That's the least we can do after you saved Ellen's and Kathleen's lives."

Lt Parker went on, "Alright, sir, it's a bargain! We'll come back as soon as we can."

Ellen ordered, "Make sure you replace our wine."

"Yes, ma'am."

The trooper was fast asleep before Ellen finished sewing and bandaging him up. Homer and Arthur fixed a pallet on the floor in the living room for him. Once Ellen was ready, the troopers moved him to the pallet where he would be more comfortable.

The sergeant asked, "Ma'am, where can we string the bear up, so we can have him for supper?"

"There's a couple of big trees behind the barn you can use."

Grace said in relief, "I'm glad the bear wasn't the cub's mama we saw earlier."

Lt Parker responded, "The cub's mama was around

close, so don't worry about the cub."

The Murphy families and the Union troopers had supper together that evening. The men talked about their homes, loved ones, and enjoyed Harry's story about the kittens. Here they were in the middle of a war from opposite sides, but the situation didn't matter to any of them. Lt Parker was leaving his wounded trooper in the care of a Confederate family, but he knew the family would be kind to his man and honorable. The lieutenant knew his company had to catch the escaped deserters before they hurt or killed innocent civilians. The deserters were a ruthless bunch that would kill anybody, because war gave them a chance to murder for no reason.

The following morning, the Union troopers headed out early, determined to complete their mission. For the Murphy family, they started repairing the storm damage and caring for the wounded soldier. Life went on for both sides no matter what happened. Homer and Arthur went to work building a new outhouse.

Civil War brogans

The Murphy family went to work, because there were more jobs to do than normal. Homer had enough boards in the barn to repair the chicken house roof and build a new outhouse. However, that left none to repair the fences. This problem would require a creative touch.

Kathleen and Andy picked the garden, because Ellen was canning for the winter months.

Teddy and Grace were assigned the chicken house repairs while Ty and Leann took a wagon to the fields to bring in the crops. Deidre and Harry went to work on the apple tree.

Within ten days, the outhouse was in business, the chicken house roof was fixed, Ellen had canned lots of food, and the apple tree was almost bare. A lot of apples went to make apple cider.

Homer commented, "Well, the water has gone down, so we can repair the wagon road."

Arthur chimed in, "That shouldn't take us too long to fix. I'm sure I'll get blisters on my hands."

Homer laughed and went on, "You need to toughen up your hands. I'm leaving the fences until last, because the fallen trees cover the fences where they fell, anyway."

"That's a good idea. I checked Harry's path through the woods to get to the river. It's not flooded, just kind of muddy here and there."

Homer smiled and said, "That rascal has been after me to let him go fishing."

Arthur suggested, "We need to check on our supplies, anyway. Why don't the three of us go fishing? You and I can start on the wagon road, tomorrow."

"Sounds like a plan to me. A mess of fish will taste mighty good. Let's go git the rascal and head out."

The threesome headed out to the river hoping to catch lots of fish for supper. The path was soggy in places, but they got to the river with no trouble.

Harry blabbed, "Let's have a contest! The one who catches the most fish gits an extra piece of Mama's apple pie."

Arthur responded, "That's a deal, you rascal!"

So, the race was on to determine a winner. All three were catching fish and staying neck and neck. Harry hooked on to a big one, and managed to pull it in.

Homer shouted, "That's a huge one, son. You git to eat that one!"

Just then, Arthur shouted, "Get over here, Homer! I need your help!"

Homer and Harry ran over to Arthur wondering what in the world was going on.

Harry blabbed, "I bet Uncle Arthur has caught a big one!"

They looked where Arthur was pointing.

Homer replied, "Sweet Jesus! I wonder how long he's been here? His body got tangled up in the tree roots and bushes."

"Could he be one of the Yankee deserters the lieutenant was after?"

Homer answered, "Who knows. Let's git him pulled over here and check his clothes."

When the men got the dead Yankee on dry land, they examined him.

Arthur suggested, "He appears to be in his twenties,

has two bullets holes in his back, and he's wearing brogans, so he's probably an infantryman and not cavalry."

Homer continued, "Here's a pocket watch, a leather bag full of Yankee gold and silver coins, and a pouch. Let's see what's in it."

Harry shouted, "Look at all that jewelry. It's really pretty! There's rings, necklaces, and pins. Where did he git them from?"

Homer answered, "I'm thinking he stole all of it."

"Does any of it look familiar?"

Homer thought and said, "Not to me. Maybe, Ellen might recognize it. Harry, go back to the barn and git two shovels. Don't say anything about this just yet."

"Don't worry, Poppa!"

Harry raced through the woods, got the shovels out of the barn, and high tailed it back to the river.

Arthur studied the corpse and said, "He doesn't have a canteen, knapsack, and any weapons or ammunition. Don't you think that's odd?"

Homer added, "Not all of that gear would have washed off his body. Obviously, his cap did. Letters and pictures could have been lost, too."

Harry chimed in, "He don't have a sword or knife, neither!"

Arthur continued, "He's not an officer, and there are no stripes on his sleeves, so he must be a private."

Homer shook his head and stated, "I'm tired of burying dead soldiers. Let's bury him in the woods. I don't want to drag him to our graveyard of unknowns."

Arthur replied, "I agree."

Harry suggested, "That deserter could have stolen those things from Fredericksburg."

"We'll show them to all the women and see if they recognize any of the pieces."

When the men finished burying the soldier, they decided they had enough fish for a good supper. The threesome went back to the house, cleaned the fish, and washed up.

They got the ladies together and showed them the jewelry. No one could remember seeing any of the pieces. Homer showed the wounded trooper the pocket watch and bag of coins. He had no idea where they came from. He told them to keep what they found, because he wasn't one of their deserters.

The next day while Homer and Arthur worked on the wagon road, familiar faces came riding up the road with a wagon.

Lt Parker greeted, "I'm glad to see you, again. How is my wounded trooper?"

Homer answered, "He's much better, but not able to ride a horse yet."

"That's why I brought along a wagon."

Arthur asked, "What on earth is in the wagon, Lieutenant?"

"We brought you some things you might need."

"We're doing alright," Homer mentioned.

Lt Parker commented, "It's kind of a gift for taking care of my trooper."

"You don't need to do that," Homer responded.

Lt Parker suggested, "No arguments, Mr. Murphy and Judge Murphy. You have to take the supplies, or there won't be any room for my trooper."

Homer threw up his arms and said, "Alright, I surrender. Let's git to the house."

Ellen saw blue uniforms on horseback and was about ready to get her shotgun, but she recognized them as they got closer. When they rode up to the porch, she put her hands on her hips and asked, "Did you catch them varmints, Lt Hound Dog?"

"We certainly did, because my company is the best. We took them back to Fredericksburg. They'll be facing a firing squad one day."

"Your trooper is coming along quite well. I took the thread out of him last night, but he's not up to no fighting just yet."

The trooper hobbled onto the porch and saluted.

Lt Parker commented, "You sure do look better, private."

"Sir, I feel a lot better, just sore as the devil!"

The sergeant said, "We brought a wagon to take you back to Fredericksburg. Of course, we have to unload the supplies first."

Ellen asked, "What supplies?"

The sergeant answered, "The supplies for you as a gift for taking care of Pvt Owens."

Ellen asked, "Homer, what's going on here?"

He responded, "Don't argue with the lieutenant, because it won't do any good."

Harry ran up to the lieutenant and shouted, "Hi, Lt Hound Dog!"

He replied, "Well, I'll be, it's Hush Up Harry!"

"I've been good and busy. We got lots of things to repair and crops that need picking. I'm the apple picker."

"I'm proud you're helping your family."

Lt Parker looked at Ellen and said, "We've brought you flour, cornmeal, sugar, salt, coffee, and feed for the livestock and chickens."

The sergeant chimed in, "Ma'am, the men chipped in and got you a basket of sweet potatoes and four bottles of wine."

Deidre commented, "Oh, I love sweet potatoes with butter and honey spread on them!"

Lt Parker continued, "To top it off, we killed two deer on the way here, so you can enjoy venison for supper."

The troopers started unloading the supplies, and Ellen told them where to put them.

Lt Parker added, "I have passes here signed by my division commander for you and Mr. Arthur. It allows you to get through Union lines to get food and supplies you might need from our commissary and medical help, if you need it."

Homer responded, "We really appreciate what you've done for us!"

Arthur asked, "Did you have time to check on our homes?"

"Yes, sir. All three homes are being used as officer's quarters. They don't seem to be damaged."

Arthur remarked, "Thank you for checking."

Lt Parker ordered, "Trooper Owens get your things, so we can get you back to Fredericksburg. We can't enjoy a meal with you Mrs. Murphy, because we have to get back as soon as possible."

"I understand. You have been mighty nice to us. We pray ya'll will remain safe and return home well," Ellen said.

Lt Parker added, "Even though your sons are in the Confederate army, we pray they will return home, safely. Godspeed to all of you!"

Pvt Owens said, "I'll never forget your kindness, Ms. Ellen. I'll pray for your family's safety."

Ellen blabbed, "Leave the darn bears alone, because they hate Yankees!"

He replied, "I'll remember that. Godspeed, ma'am."

Homer, Arthur, and the boys shook each trooper's hand.

Lt Parker patted Harry's head and said, "May we meet again one day when we're on the same side."

As the Union soldier's rode away, the women wiped tears along with Harry.

Harry asked, "Why are you crying, Mama?"

"I'm not crying! I just have something in my eye."

He replied, "But   ."

Leann cut him off and said, "Hush up, Harry!"

He thought, "I'll never understand crying women!"

Amid all the insanity between the North and the South, a few acts of kindness still existed.

Hardtack

CHAPTER 15

The Battle of Globe Tavern was fought between August 18ᵗʰ and August 21ˢᵗ. The Second Battle of Ream's Station occurred on August 25, 1864. It only closed part of the Weldon Railroad to the Confederates. Gen Grant wanted the railroad captured and controlled, completely. He assigned Gen Hancock's II Corps and a cavalry division the task of capturing the rail line.

Second Battle of Ream's Station

On August 23ʳᵈ, the cavalry division and one infantry division from Hancock's II Corps destroyed tracks until they were only two miles away from Ream's Station. The following day another Union infantry division occupied Ream's Station.

Gen Lee knew he needed to run the Union forces out of the station. If Dinwiddie Court House fell into Yankee hands, Lee would have to evacuate Richmond and Petersburg. If Gen Lee could whip the Union army here, it would affect northern morale and the presidential election in November.

Gen Lee chose his III Corps commander to carry out the expedition; however, Gen A. P. Hill was ill, so he assigned Gen Heth the command.

By August 24th, three miles of tracks were destroyed south of Ream's Station by Hancock's II Corps. The following day Confederate forces marched down the Dinwiddie Stage Road. By 2:00 pm, the battle was on between Hancock's boys and the Confederates.

This day would haunt Gen Hancock for the rest of his life, because some of his troops refused to fight and others bolted in panic leaving holes in the Union line by late afternoon. Gen Hancock rode among his men begging them to hold their positions. Finally, he was able to mount a counterattack, and this gave his troops time to withdraw back to Petersburg in the darkness.

It was a Confederate victory, but they weren't able to retake the 16 miles of track south of Petersburg. So, the supplies Gen Lee needed for his army had to be moved by wagon trains.

In mid-September, Archer's brigade, including the 47th Virginia, started building trenches about a half a mile in front and alongside of the Boydton Plank Road. Another line of trenches was built along the Squirrel Level Road. These trenches also contained three forts.

The one hundred and sixty-two men in the regiment would be so glad when they didn't have to dig a trench, ever again.

When the brigade found out the Union had broken through some of the outer defenses in Richmond, they were ordered to march north towards Petersburg. That evening the brigade camped near Battery 45.

The brigade thought they were headed to Richmond, but Gen Grant had other plans.

The Union objective was to capture the Squirrel Level and Boydton Plank Roads, so they could cut the South Side Railroad. Losing the railroad would cut off supplies and food from reaching Gen Lee's army.

On September 30th, Gen Warren's V Corps and a cavalry division had started towards the Poplar Springs and the Squirrel Level Roads. By 1:00 pm, Union troops slammed into Confederate forces near Poplar Springs Church and captured Fort Archer. The few Rebel forces in the trenches along the Squirrel Level Line withdrew, quickly.

Gen Warren stopped, because he wanted to fortify his position and not get too far ahead of the IX Corps.

Archer's brigade was recalled from Battery 45 and ordered to march along the Boydton Plank Road to Pegram's Farm where the enemy was fortifying their positions.

Gus asked, "Why are we going south?"

Cpl Steptoe Washington answered, "To flank the enemy position at the farm."

Gus fumed, "Good Lord Almighty, that place is nothing but a swamp, grape-vines, briars, and tangled bushes. You can't march through that, quickly!"

David added, "That wilderness can eat you up."

Sgt Patton remarked, "Do the best you can."

The 47th Virginia and the brigade stumbled through the morass to the point of exhaustion, but the leading elements were able to break through into an open area.

Those units were deployed, but the Virginia regiments were still struggling through the swamp.

When Archer's brigade got out of the swamp, they were ordered to follow the Church Road to Pegram's Farm. When they got to the battlefield, they attacked the right position of the Union forces. As they marched, they were hit with a withering volley from the Yanks.

The captain yelled, "Hold your ground, men!"

Aaron reloaded, aimed, and fired.

A soldier in front of Aaron was hit in the head, and Aaron was sprayed with blood and flesh. He wiped his face as he stepped over the dead soldier.

David was relieved to know Aaron wasn't hit. He saw fellow soldiers drop all along the line. He reloaded, aimed, and fired as quickly as he could.

Clay's musket wouldn't fire, so he grabbed another one.

Suddenly, Rebels and Yanks were fighting hand-to-hand. Gus jumped a young Yankee and stabbed him in the throat. Micah drove his bayonet into a corporal. Clay wrestled with a tall Yank and drove his knife in his back several times. David saw a Yank coming up behind Gus, so David launched himself at the Yank. The two wrestled on the ground putting every ounce of energy into the combat. David was able to stab the Yank's arm. The soldier in blue screamed, and that gave David time to stab him with a mortal blow.

A young Yank who couldn't be over sixteen charged towards Micah with his bayonet, but Micah was able to dodge the bayonet and trip the Yank. Micah jumped on his back and stabbed him several times. The combat went on for about thirty minutes when Yankee artillery opened fire on the Confederates, and they were ordered to withdraw to the Jones Farm. When they reached the area, they set up a battle line.

Aaron laid on the ground exhausted, sore, hungry, and thirsty. There were two bullet holes in his uniform. Micah was tired and the knife wound on his leg was painful. He rolled up his pants leg and knew he needed medical help.

Cpl Steptoe ordered, "Pvt Johnson get that taken care of at the surgeon's tent."

Micah limped to the rear knowing he was lucky this day, so far.

Gus looked at his hat and commented, "Sweet Jesus, there's a bullet hole in it!"

Clay fired back, "Good Lord, that was mighty close. You sure you have all your hair?"

Gus felt around and said, "Yep!"

Around 9:00 pm, a storm rolled in, the rain poured, and the men found shelter wherever they could.

David commented, "It seems like every time we're in battle it rains."

Aaron responded, "The rain is trying to wash the blood away from this place."

The men huddled together under some large trees and drifted off to sleep. For a little while, the savage fighting drifted away as the men slept despite the rain.

On October 1st around 3:00 am, the men were ordered back to Battery 45. The march back was dreadful, because it was made in the dark on a crowded, muddy road.

Gen Heth had his division marching back down the Squirrel Level Road at sunrise. The men deployed in battle ranks in an open field east of the road, and Archer's brigade sent out skirmishers. Around 7:00 am, the skirmishers found Union skirmishers in a wooded area between the Chappell Farm and the Davis house.

As the brigade pressed forward into the woods, they ran into a North Carolina brigade withdrawing from an earlier attack on Fort Britton. Another regiment and brigade collided with the North Carolinians. There was mass confusion, and this time a southern battalion refused to advance! Even the officers refused to move.

It started to rain as Archer's brigade marched out of the woods into heavy Union fire. The brigade pulled back and got caught up in the retreating regiments. The brigade stayed in the woods until Gen Heth ordered them to return to their Petersburg earthworks at nightfall.

The Confederates lost the Squirrel Level Road, but they held on to the Boydton Plank Road line. The South Side Railroad remained in southern hands.

The 47th Virginia suffered one killed in action. Capt Jordan Ware from Co. K was killed on October 1, 1864.

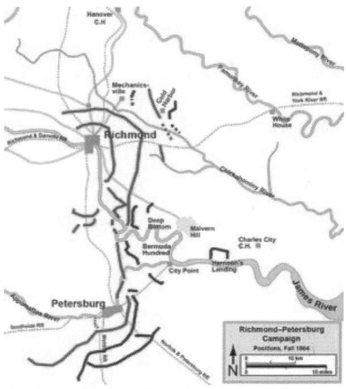

Richmond-Petersburg Campaign Fall 1864

In early October, Archer's brigade was ordered to take over the trenches on the Boydton Plank Road line near Church Road. Of course, the men were back at their favorite pastime of digging trenches and picket duty. Later, they were moved to the right and continued digging and fortifying trenches and pulling picket duty.

The brigade lost Gen Archer when he died on October 24th. Again, Col Mayo was given command of the brigade, and Capt Wharton became the commanding officer of the 47th Virginia.

The Battle of Burgess Mill was fought on October 27th

and 28th. Gen Grant wanted to capture the Boydton
Plank Road and the South Side Railroad. This would
stop supplies getting to the Rebel army.

Again, Gen Grant chose Gen Hancock's II Corps, parts
of the V and IX corps, and a cavalry division to take part
in the attack.

Gen Hancock marched his corps across Hatcher's Run
and headed towards Burgess Mill.

Gen A. P. Hill was too sick to command his corps, so
Gen Heth directed the III Corps. The two divisions
Gen Heth put in front of Gen Hancock were easily
pushed out of their trenches. Other Union elements
failed to hook up with Gen Hancock, so the II Corps
found itself isolated north of Hatcher's Run and
surrounded on three sides. However, this time
Hancock's men didn't panic and went on the offensive.
Hancock would turn the tables on the Confederates and
almost encircle them.

In the end, the Confederates still held the Boydton
Plank Road and the South Side Railroad.

Col Mayo's brigade held the trenches close to
Hatcher's Run, so they didn't take part in the battle
which saved them from suffering casualties. It was
probably a good thing, because the brigade was wearing
a lot of Union uniforms, because their uniforms were
close to rags.

November would be a rough month on the brigade,
because the rainy cold days made picket and guard duty
difficult.

On November 29th, the brigade was inspected, and
the results were not good. The inspector found military
appearance, discipline, and instruction lax. Regimental

commanders were indifferent and had little interest in their commands. The
47th Virginia was still rated good for a clean camp, personal cleanliness, and were well instructed on guard and picket duty. The inspector noted the shortage of food, uniforms, weapons, and feed for its animals.

At this point, the 47th Virginia had ten officers and one hundred and fifty-five men present for duty. Col Mayo commanded the brigade, and command of the 47th Virginia was given to Capt Charles Green.

Clay commented, "I think these inspections are a waste of time, because all they do is tell us something we already know."

Gus asked, "How can we look soldierly if we have to steal uniforms from the Yanks or our dead?"

David fumed, "I say the army needs to send us uniforms and shoes when we need them."

Micah fumed, "They git on us for not having enough bayonets and such. Then, why doesn't the army send us what we need?"

Aaron fussed, "We need overcoats and gloves, but I don't see any being passed out for the winter."

Clay remarked, "I love the one about our animals being poorly fed. Where is the feed for them?"

In December, Gen Grant ordered more tracks destroyed on the Weldon Railroad further south. Col Mayo's brigade and the III Corps were ordered to stop the Yankees. The brigade left on December 8th and would end up marching a hundred miles many times in the sleet and freezing rain. Gen Heth gave up chasing the Union raiders, because the men were worn out, footsore, and the roads were nothing but mud.

By December 13th, the brigade collapsed in their trenches near Hatcher's Run.

David fumed, "That was a waste of time. We marched our shoes off for nothing!"

Gus fussed, "It's a wonder all of us don't have pneumonia!"

Aaron looked at Micah and said, "I'm glad your knife wound had time to heal before we went out on that wild goose chase."

"Me, too. At least, we managed to steal some clothes and shoes from the Yanks."

Clay added, "All of us got gloves thanks to the Yanks."

David commented, "Lord, how I miss my wife and son!"

Aaron remarked, "All I want is to hold my wife in my arms and tell her how much I love her."

Micah stated, "I pray Grace will still love and marry me."

David teased, "You don't have to worry about that. What Grace said came from her heart."

Clay mentioned, "I miss the farm, my parents, and even Ty and Harry. Those two rascals are good boys. Leann is the sister we never had."

Gus added, "They are good brothers. Shoot fire! They keep Mama going, and Leann is wonderful for Mama."

David remarked, "I pray they're safe and have enough to eat."

Clay continued, "I hope we have a Christmas truce, so we don't have to worry about sharpshooters."

Gus fired back, "Amen to that! We need to get out of this dungeon for a day. When the trenches start closing in on me, I look at the sky and think about green grass and green leaves."

Micah laughed and said, "I think about geese flying and eating one for dinner."

David chimed in, "I think about kissing my wife and son."

Micah asked, "How about you, Aaron?"

"I think about kissing Deidre in front of the fireplace."

Micah asked, "How about you, Clay?"

"I think about fishing in the river and bringing home a mess of fish for supper."

David asked, "How about you, Cpl Steptoe?"

"I think about finding some moonshine and drinking my fill."

The men laughed and retreated into their own world of happy thoughts. If they didn't, they would go crazy.

The men would spend Christmas in the trenches. There were no presents, no tree, or lots of good food to eat. The men were only issued a little more rations. Some of the men sang some Christmas carols. Most of the men wondered if they would survive 1865 and finally go home.

The day after Christmas the men from the 47th Virginia, the 55th Virginia, the 40th Virginia, and the 22nd Virginia Battalion were told to get their belongings, because they were headed to the Richmond defenses north of the James River near Chaffin's Bluff. This area was well-fortified and saw little action. They were assigned to the II Corps under the command of Gen Richard Ewell. Their division commander was Gen G. W. Custis Lee, and their brigade commander was Gen Seth Barton from Fredericksburg.

Even though they were only five miles from Richmond, they were still suffering from little food and worn out uniforms.

Gen Seth Barton   Gen G. W. Custis Lee

On a bitter, cold day in January 1865, the friends were waking up knowing their scarecrow breakfast wouldn't stop their hunger.

Gus poked Clay to wake him up, but didn't get any response.

Gus shouted, "Wake up, Clay!"

He crawled over to him and knew something was wrong.

Clay whispered, "I can't breathe, Gus. I feel mighty bad!"

Gus felt him, and Clay was burning up with fever.

He yelled, "Help me, boys! We got to git Clay to the doctor!"

David said, "I'll carry him. Come on, Clay. We're taking you to git help."

The friends rushed Clay to the hospital tent as quickly as they could. They moved him inside the warmed tent and put him on a cot.

Gus yelled, "You got to help him, Doc!"

Shortly, the doctor came over to the friends with a blank look on his face.

He said, "I'm sorry, he has pneumonia, and there's nothing I can do for him."

Gus grabbed the doctor's coat and yelled, "My brother was fine yesterday! You have to do something!"

"Your brother's lungs are full of fluid, and that's why he's having trouble breathing."

Gus got up in the doctor's face and shouted, "You listen to me, you butcher! Do something for him!"

David pulled Gus over to Clay's cot and said, "You need to be with him! He needs you!"

Gus grabbed Clay's hand, knelt by his cot, and wept a river of tears.

Clay whispered, "Tell Mama and Poppa I love them. Tell them I did my duty for Virginia and the Confederacy."

Gus mumbled between tears, "You're going to get better!"

"No, my brother. I know my time is near. I'm so very tired."

Clay coughed and gasped for air.

Clay whispered, "It's so dark. Don't leave me, Gus!"

"I'm right here, Clay."

Clay's head rolled to the side, and his face turned ashen white. Gus gathered him up in his arms and cried. The friends gave Gus time with his brother while they said their farewells in their own way. Clay had a cough like everyone else in the regiment, but he never complained he was feeling, poorly. It was so fast, but, maybe, that was a good thing.

The doctor told the friends he hated losing any

patients, but there just wasn't anything he could do.

Finally, Gus laid his brother on the cot, took his knife, and pocket watch. The friends watched as Gus walked out of the tent, found a shovel, and proceeded to dig a grave for his brother.

David walked over and said, "Let us help you, Gus."

"Leave me alone! I must do this by myself!"

David decided Gus had to deal with his sorrow in his own way. Clay knew he was dying, and David knew in his heart the end was coming for the Confederacy. They were starving and running out of supplies. Now, Clay wasn't suffering anymore like so many were. He was in a far better place than they were. Would they all die before the war was over? Would Virginia become an enormous graveyard and a ravaged, desolate land?

The friends kept their distance while Gus buried his beloved brother. When he finished, he sat next to the grave and just stared.

Micah asked, "What should we do? He can't sit out here all day, or he'll end up with pneumonia!"

David suggested, "Let's go over and pay our respects."

David stood next to Gus and said, "Clay was a fine man and soldier, and we'll all miss him."

Gus jumped up and started beating on David's chest.

Gus yelled, "Clay was the good son! I was always getting into trouble! I should be in that grave, not him!"

Aaron and Micah pulled Gus away from David.

David looked into Gus's eyes and said, "Now it's your time to be the good son, so you can make him and your family proud of you!"

Aaron said, "All of us are here to help you, so don't give up! Somehow, we are going to make it through this war together!"

"Forgive me David, I'm so sorry. It's not your fault Clay died!"

Aaron commented, "Remember, Sgt Watson fought bad colds and coughs while we marched up and down the Shenandoah Valley in snow, sleet, rain, and cold winds."

Micah continued, "I don't know why all of us don't have pneumonia or dia-ree. We're still losing men because of the runs."

David suggested, "Let's get our scarecrow breakfast and try to stay warm."

Gus mentioned, "I'm giving Harry Clay's hat and Ty Clay's knife. Micah, you can wear Clay's jacket. The rest of his uniform and clothes are falling apart. His shoes are full of holes. We'll divide up his ammunition and give Sgt Steptoe his musket, because he'll know if someone needs it."

Micah added, "Clay liked it here by the James River. He liked looking at the river, because it made him feel at peace."

Aaron looked at Clay's soldier grave and said, "Godspeed good friend. You will always be in our hearts."

Micah added, "Godspeed Clay. I'll always remember all the good times we spent together."

The four friends walked away wondering what the future and fate had in store for them.

CHAPTER 16

On February 5th, the Union tried to capture the Boydton Plank Road and the Weldon Railroad west of Petersburg. Although the Union failed to capture both, they were able to extend their fortified trenches to the Vaughn Road crossing at Hatcher's Run. The Rebels fought bravely to keep the vital Boydton Plank Road open, but they had to dig more trenches which thinned their lines even more.

The 47th Virginia and its brigade were not involved in this attack, so they were spared any casualties.

The Union would suffer almost 1,600 casualties compared to Confederate losses set at almost 1,200 men.

In late March, Gen Lee's army was weakened by disease, desertions, and lack of food and supplies. He knew he was outnumbered over two to one.

Gen Lee looked at his situation and considered Gen John B. Gordon's recommendations. They could offer peace terms to the Union, abandon Richmond and Petersburg and join up with Gen Joseph Johnston's army in North Carolina, or fight. Gen Lee decided to fight.

Gen John B. Gordon was given the command of Gen Lee's last offensive action of the war.

Confederate forces attacked Union troops at Fort Stedman on March 25th in the early morning. Attacks went back and forth between the two sides for four hours, but Gen Gordon wasn't able to capture Fort Stedman, hold it, or gain any ground.

The Union would suffer almost 1,100 casualties

compared to Confederate losses set at 4,000 men.
Gen Lee's position was weakened, he lost valuable men
he couldn't replace, and he couldn't break the Union
stranglehold.

Gen John B. Gordon   Bombproof at Fort Stedman

George, Luella, and Eva Moss got into their wagon
and headed towards Homer's farm for a visit. It seemed
like an eternity since their sons marched off to war, and
they enjoyed picnics together. Their son, Abner,
wouldn't be coming home, because he had given his life
for Virginia.

Eva was their only surviving child. George was a
blacksmith and wheelwright who couldn't continue to
live in Fredericksburg, because he couldn't find work.
So many people fled to get away from exploding shells,
bullets, fire, looting, and the enemy on their doorstep.
George had no idea if his home was still there or not.

Now, he and his family were living near Bowling
Green where he was making enough of a living to
survive. Of course, Confederate money was worthless,
so folks had to resort to using the barter system. Also,

he had some Union gold and silver coins stashed away just in case he became desperate.

George and Luella had lost contact with Micah's parents after they moved to Lancaster on the Northern Neck. The Johnson family had lost their home in Fredericksburg, because it was looted and burned by the Yankees. The Battle of Fredericksburg destroyed so much of the town as well as the surrounding area.

George wondered how were the surrounding counties going to rebuild and get back to normal. This part of Virginia was almost a wasteland. How were people going to make a living and feed their families? Oh well, the only way to find out was to live each day the best they could and help each other. If the Confederacy lost the war, Virginia would survive and rise up out of the ashes of devastation, because Virginians had that tough settler, pioneer spirit running through their veins.

Eva asked, "Poppa, you are mighty quiet. Is there something wrong?"

He answered, "I was just thinking about how tough Virginians will need to be when the war is over."

She responded, "They might force us to raise the white flag, but the North will never break our spirit!"

Luella shot back, "You are so right, honey!"

When George got near the Murphy home, the families ran out to greet them. It was such a wonderful feeling to see close friends, spend time with them, and enjoy a meal together even though they might not have all the extra trimmings. They could get away from the war for a short while and just concentrate on each other.

Ellen commented, "Lordy Eva, you sure have

changed! You're not that awkward, skinny girl anymore. Your hair is beautiful, you're pretty as a picture, and all filled out in all the right places, I might add!"

Eva blushed and said, "Thank you, Ms. Ellen."

Kathleen added, "You look like a true southern belle, honey!"

Deidre asked, "How old are you, now?"

"I'm nineteen."

Harry blabbed, "I'd marry you if I wasn't too young. You're mighty pretty."

"Thank you, Harry. I appreciate that compliment."

Eva saw Deidre with a baby and asked, "Oh, isn't she a beautiful child. What's her name?"

"Belle."

How old is she?"

"She's seven months," answered Deidre.

Homer jumped in and said, "Deidre took in Belle, because she was an orphaned child."

Luella remarked, "Well, that was the Christian thing to do! There are so many children that have been orphaned all over the South. It breaks my heart wondering what is going to happen to them?"

Deidre breathed a sigh of relief, because the story seemed to satisfy them. She didn't want to go into any details about Belle, because the less said the better.

Ellen suggested, "Come on in the house, so we can visit. Then, I'll fix you a good meal from last year's crops."

George was surprised about the cavalry skirmish on Homer's land. Luella commented she would have fainted when those Yankees searched the house.

The Moss family wasn't surprised at the damage

Homer suffered from the bad August storm in 1864. Everybody had a big laugh over the outhouse explosion, and Ty's narrow escape from all the flying poop and wood.

Arthur and Homer didn't mention the bear incident, but the Moss family was mighty alarmed at the four Confederate deserters.

Eva looked at Leann and said, "I don't know if I could have been that brave. That was quick thinking that saved the day!"

Harry blabbed, "We took care of them varmints!"

"Hush up, Harry," Grace warned.

He replied, "That's my nickname, Eva."

"That's just perfect for you!"

George remarked, "Teddy, it was a good thing you were in the barn. I didn't know you were that good with a bow and arrow."

Teddy responded, "It takes too long to reload a gun. I'm much faster with the bow."

Harry and Grace went on to tell them about his kittens. He had named the male kitten, Flash, and the female kitten, Bonnie.

Ty got his banjo out and the families sang songs and danced before the women put a delicious meal together. Thank heavens, Homer and Arthur had killed a deer that morning and had trapped some rabbits and squirrels.

When the Moss family left, all of them felt better and their spirits were lifted. The short time they spent together gave them hope and wonderful memories during this time of suffering and madness.

When the Confederate forces failed to capture Fort Stedman, Gen Lee realized he couldn't defend Richmond and Petersburg by dividing his army. Also, he realized Gen Grant would keep going after the South Side Railroad and the Boydton Plank Road. This was a vital supply and communication route for the Confederacy.

The Battle of Lewis's Farm on March 29, 1865 was a Union success, because the Confederate troops lost control of the Boydton Plank Road. The Confederates pulled back to the White Oak Road which was their most important line of entrenchments.

On March 30th and 31st, the sky opened up with pouring rain turning the trenches to mud. The Battle of Lewis's Farm would be the beginning of Gen Grant's Appomattox Campaign.

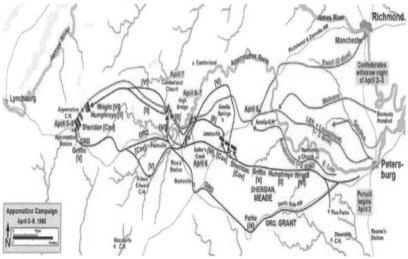

Appomattox Campaign April 2-9, 1865

The Battle of Sutherland's Station on April 2nd was a Union victory, because the Yankees gained control of Confederate entrenchments between Hatcher's Run and the Boydton Plank Road. Then, the Union was able to capture the South Side Railroad cutting off Gen Lee's last supply route into Petersburg. However, Gen Lee had enough time to withdraw his forces that night from Richmond and Petersburg. During this time, Confederate Gen A. P. Hill was killed, and Gen Lee would have to replace him with Gen Richard Anderson.

On April 2nd, the 47th Virginia and Gen Ewell's II Corps were ordered to withdraw from their lines in Richmond and head west abandoning their capital. As fate would have it, Gen Barton's brigade ended up being the rear guard. The brigade of about 1,300 men were given one day's rations for the march. The men left their trenches at 2:00 am April 3rd. They crossed the James River on the Wilton pontoon bridge and marched west through Chesterfield County. Gen Lee's army was supposed to head to Amelia Court House where supplies and food were waiting for them.

The brigade marched 17 dreadful miles before they camped at Tomahawk Church.

Aaron complained, "How can we get to Amelia Court House if the road stays clogged with people fleeing Richmond?"

David responded, "The poor people are terrified and want to get away."

Gus added, "The refugees look as bad as we do. Their clothes are worn and tattered, their eyes are sunken in, and their hair is dirty and unkempt."

Micah continued, "The poor kids are barefoot, dirty, and hungry."

David mentioned, "Their faces show despair and fear."

Aaron asked, "Where did the naval personnel come from?"

Micah answered, "They have to be the James River Squadron. Somebody said there were about 350 of them."

Gus suggested, "I hope they know how to fire a musket, because they're infantry, now."

While part of Gen Lee's army tried to reach Amelia Court House on clogged roads, the Union cavalry attacked Rebel rear guard troops at Namozine Church and Willicomack Creek.

Capt Thomas Custer, brother to Gen George Armstrong Custer, captured three Confederate officers, eleven enlisted men, and the battle flag of the 2nd North Carolina Cavalry. He would be awarded his first Medal of Honor. The Union cavalry captured around 300 prisoners, about 100 horses, and an artillery piece. They had cleared the road to Namozine Church of Confederate troops.

The brigade started marching before dawn in a light rain on April 4th headed towards Amelia Court House that was 39 miles from Richmond. When they reached the Appomattox River, there was no pontoon bridge to cross. They had to go further down the river and cross the Mattoax railroad bridge. The crossing was dangerous, because the men had to walk on wet planks laid across the rails. After they crossed, the brigade camped for the night. There would be no rations, because there were none.

Union Gen Philip Sheridan's cavalry captured Jetersville, Burkeville, and skirmished with Confederate troops at Tabernacle Church and Amelia Court House.

Now, Gen Lee was cut off from using the Richmond and Danville Railroad to escape southwestward.

On April 5th, the brigade started marching before dawn on the clogged road full of refugees, broken down wagons, and retreating troops. Exhausted and broken down soldiers littered the sides of the road.

Aaron said, "I'm so hungry I'd eat my shoes if I had any. Darn my feet hurt like the devil!"

David stated, "I hope we get rations soon before all of us collapse from hunger."

Micah remarked, "I hope there's some shoes in those supplies, because mine are now gone. Well, at least, I'm not walking in snow or sleet."

What the friends didn't know was the 200 Confederate wagons full of food and supplies took the wrong road and were destroyed by Yankee cavalry. When the brigade reached Amelia Court House and found out there was no food waiting, the worn out men were furious. Barton's brigade was down to 500 exhausted, starving men.

Gus shouted, "How do they expect us to fight the Yanks when we haven't had rations in three days? The first time I see a commissary soldier I'm wringing his neck!"

Aaron shouted, "The Yankee cavalry is barking at our tails just like at Gettysburg. It won't be long before the Yankee infantry will be breathing down our necks."

Sgt Steptoe said, "Gen Lee has ordered us to march through the night towards Farmville to look for food."

David asked, "How far is Farmville from here?"

"About 25 miles."

David yelled, "We can't march that far in one day.

We're starving and exhausted!"

The sergeant said, "Just remember, if you fall out on the side of the road, you'll end up in a Yankee prison."

Micah snapped, "We'll keep that in mind, Sgt Steptoe."

The men marched through the night dead on their feet. They stopped for a while collapsing on the ground. Micah's feet were bleeding, and every step was like walking on fire. Aaron's feet were in the same shape as Micah's. Gus felt like he was walking in the desert one moment and in the jagged mountains the next. David kept thinking about Kathleen, Andy, and his family. He tried to make his mind think they were in Farmville waiting for them.

Petersburg trenches left behind

CHAPTER 17

On April 6th, the brigade continued to marching towards Farmville. They reached a place called Sailor's Creek around 3:00 pm, and firing started ahead and behind them. Union forces had managed to cut Gen Richard Ewell's II Corps off from the rest of Gen Lee's army in this swampy bottomland.

Orders were shouted for Gen Custis Lee's division to set up on the left side of the road. The 47th Virginia was in the center of the line. This time they were facing Union cavalry, infantry, and artillery. The artillery fired several rounds first, and then, the infantry and cavalry charged.

Battle of Sailor's Creek April 6, 1865

That kick of adrenaline hit the friends, and they entered their world of combat being one with their weapon. The Union troops ran into a wall of horrendous fire from the Confederates and were forced to fall back. The Union artillery resumed fire, and a shell exploded near the friends. Aaron screamed out in excruciating pain, because a piece of shrapnel had hit him below the elbow, and he couldn't feel his hand. David grabbed him and cradled his brother in his arms. He had an old scarf, so he wrapped it around his arm above the elbow, tightly. Poor Aaron shook from pain and floated in and out of consciousness.

For David, things started moving in slow motion. He saw a Yankee cavalryman grab the 40th Virginia's battle flag. Then, he saw LtCol Bruce and Capt Wharton captured. The Union troops swarmed into their battle lines in overwhelming numbers.

Micah yelled into David's ear, "I'm not dying in some Yankee prison! You take Aaron and follow me!"

Micah grabbed Gus and the four took off for the woods. If they were shot in the back, so be it.

Suddenly, David was hit in the hip, the thigh, and fell to the ground with Aaron in his arms. The woods was spinning and the pain was so severe.

"I got to get up and carry Aaron away from this place."

Gus yelled at Micah, "Put me down, so I can help David. You grab Aaron!"

At this point, Micah and Gus knew they were better off than the other two. They stumbled through the trees and swampy bottomlands as best as they could.

Micah heard movement and dropped to the ground followed by Gus. Both men put their hands over their suffering friend's mouths. Shortly, three Rebel soldiers ran passed them and never looked back. Micah and Gus sucked in several deep breaths before taking off, again.

They had gone about 50 yards when they heard more commotion behind them. Again, they dropped down in the bushes to hide as two Rebel cavalrymen galloped by through the underbrush.

Micah jumped up and yelled, "Please help us! Come back!"

The cavalrymen never stopped, and Micah dropped to the ground fighting back tears.

Gus shouted, "We need to get to the road and follow it westward. Maybe, we'll run into our troops."

Finally, Micah caught sight of the road. They rested for a short spell and headed for it. The road wouldn't be as hard on their feet.

Gus thought, "If we only had a wagon, we could make better time."

With every ounce of adrenaline that was left in their bodies, Micah and Gus kept moving along the road. They tried not to hurt David and Aaron any more than they had to. Each step was excruciating and sapping their energy. They stopped for a short time struggling to breathe and gather the strength to go on.

Micah struggled to get up holding David, but his legs collapsed. Gus couldn't stand, so he tried to drag Aaron behind him. He lost his grip, collapsed, and broke out in tears.

Micah shouted, "We'll rest a while."

However, when he looked up, he saw nothing but blue uniforms coming towards them with pointed muskets.

There was no way out! All they could see were blue uniforms. Could they get back in the bushes and hide?

Several Union soldiers from the 53rd Pennsylvania Infantry gathered around the friends.

Micah begged, "Please don't shoot! We surrender! Please help my friends!"

One corporal said, "You Johnny Rebs are in a bad fix!"

Both Micah and Gus couldn't hold back their tears. They had failed their friends, and they had failed the 47th Virginia.

The corporal ordered, "Get four stretchers out here, right now!"

The Union soldiers got down on their knees, gave the men water, washed their tear-streaked faces, and gave them some hardtack.

One soldier commented, "My God, look at their feet! Their uniforms are nothing but rags!"

A second one remarked, "I can't believe these two carried their friends all this way!"

Another soldier added, "I tell you one thing. I have nothing but respect for these two. Talk about devotion. I'd fight alongside of them any time."

To the friends, the water came from the fountain of youth, and hardtack never tasted so good.

The corporal pulled out a pouch of candy and gave it to the friends.

Finally, the stretcher-bearers got there, and all of them headed for Dr. Gabriel Hayden's hospital tent.

The Union soldiers kept giving the friends water and hardtack wafers as they carried the exhausted Rebel soldiers back to their camp.

Dr. Hayden and his orderlies finished setting up their hospital tents and waited for the wounded to start arriving from Sailor's Creek.

Elisha rushed inside and announced, "Dr. Hayden, sir,

four Rebel soldiers is coming in, and theys in bad shape!"

Another orderly told Dr. Hayden there were Union casualties coming in by ambulance wagons.

Dr. Hayden looked at his fellow surgeons and said, "I'll take the Confederate soldiers, and the rest of you start treating our casualties."

"Yes, sir!"

The stretcher-bearers put Aaron and David on surgical tables, and the other two were placed on cots.

Dr. Hayden examined Aaron's arm and knew he had to amputate at the elbow. He looked at David's wound and saw an ornate knife and scabbard tucked in the back of his trousers. Elisha saw it and instantly recognized the design.

He thought, "Hush up, Harry liked to look at the one his stepbrothers and father had.

Elisha said, "Sir, I recognize the knife. Ask him his name, sir."

Gabriel asked, "Private, what's your name?"

"Private David Murphy. Please keep my knife safe. It's a special gift from my father, and all of us have one."

Gabriel knew about Elisha and the Murphy family, so he made up his mind to help these men get home, safely.

Gabriel said, "Private Murphy, I'll keep the knives safe, so don't worry. I know you're in a great deal of pain. I'll keep you comfortable during this ordeal. I don't care what color your uniforms are. Now, my orderlies will start getting you ready for surgery."

David pleaded, "Don't take my leg off."

Gabriel smiled, took David's hand, and replied, "I'm not doing anything that isn't necessary."

When David looked into the handsome doctor's

piercing blue eyes, he felt at peace.

Gabriel went over to Micah and Gus to examine their feet. He wanted to kick a dead horse, because both men's feet were in awful shape.

The corporal said, "Dr. Hayden, these two Rebs carried their friends, Lord knows, how long before they collapsed on the road."

The rest of the Union soldiers shook the friend's hands and wished them luck. Dr. Hayden had taught so many of them to be men of compassion in the middle of all this madness.

Gabriel asked, "Private, what's your name?"

"Micah Johnson, Colonel."

"Well, Pvt Johnson, I'm going to do everything possible to save your feet. As long as gangrene doesn't set in, we'll be in good shape."

Gabriel asked Gus his name and told him the same thing.

"When was the last time you ate?"

Gus answered, "When we left our trenches in Richmond, but your Yanks gave us water and hardtack when they found us."

Minnie and Jonas walked into the hospital tent to help with Dr. Hayden's patients.

Dr. Hayden looked into Micah's and Gus's eyes and asked, "All my orderlies and nurses have volunteered to take care of both Union and Confederate soldiers. Am I going to have a problem with the two of you?"

They both answered, "No, sir!"

He continued, "Minnie and Jonas follow my instructions to the letter. Your uniforms and clothing are worn out and filthy. They will be burned, because you have guests staying with you that need to leave."

Micah mentioned, "They are Virginia's finest insects, Colonel."

Gabriel laughed and said, "You will be bathed, hair washed, and beards washed or shaved. If you want a haircut just tell Jonas."

Micah asked, "What are we going to wear?"

"Southern belle dresses, of course."

Gus started laughing when he saw the devilish grin on the doctor's face. Finally, Micah caught on and laughed, too.

Minnie jumped in, "Lordy Dr. Hayden, theys might be pretty women after we cleans them up!"

Gabriel added, "I think you're right, Minnie."

"After I operate on your feet let Minnie know when you feel like eating a meal. I'm ordering double rations for you, and I want you to drink a lot of water and milk. Any questions?"

Gus commented, "Please take care of our knives, sir!"

Gabriel patted Gus's shoulder and promised, "I will. Minnie is going to tell you about her meeting with your family."

Gus was dumbfounded about the snowstorm rescue. It was unbelievable.

Dr. Hayden operated on Aaron's arm first and had no choice but to amputate his left arm at the elbow, because the piece of shrapnel that hit him crushed the bone.

Next, he had Elisha help him roll David over on his stomach. He had a spent bullet in his hip that stopped right next to his pelvic bone. He removed the bullet from his hip and the one in his upper thigh. David was a very lucky man.

Gabriel took Gus next, because he had a nasty cut on his arch. The doctor had to remove all sorts of things embedded in the chewed up flesh. Micah's feet weren't much better when Gabriel operated on him.

The four friends slipped into an exhaustive sleep which they welcomed.

The Battle of Sailor's Creek resulted in the loss of Gen Ewell's II Corps numbering about 8,000 men. Eight Confederate generals were captured four of which were Gen Seth Barton, Gen Joseph Kershaw, Gen Richard Ewell, and Gen Lee's son, Gen Custis Lee. Many men from the 47th Virginia who weren't captured or wounded fled into the woods to avoid capture. On this day, the 47th Virginia wouldn't be an organized unit. Only seven non-combatant men from the 47th Virginia were paroled at Appomattox.

Almost one hundred and ninety men were paroled at different areas in Virginia such as Ashland, Bowling Green, Richmond, and King George Court House.

Sgt William Morris from the 1st New York Cavalry was awarded the Medal of Honor for capturing the flag of the 40th Virginia Infantry.

Cpl Harris Hawthorne from the 121st New York Infantry was awarded the Medal of Honor for capturing Confederate Gen Custis Lee.

Cpl Smith Larimer from the 2nd Ohio Cavalry was awarded the Medal of Honor for capturing Confederate Gen Joseph Kershaw's headquarters flag.

Capt Thomas Custer from the 6th Michigan Cavalry

was awarded his second Medal of Honor when he leaped his horse over the enemy's works and captured two colors having his horse shot from under him while severely wounded.

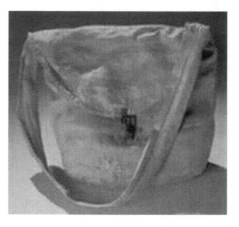

Haversacks

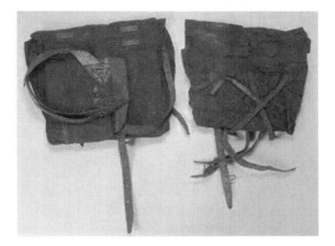

CHAPTER 18

Dr. Hayden finished in surgery, cleaned up, and ate a hearty meal. He checked with Elisha and Minnie to see how his Confederate patients were doing.

Minnie shook her head and remarked, "Doctor, sir, these four boys is almost starved to death. You can sees their ribs, and they has no meat on their bones!"

Gabriel remarked, "I know, Minnie. That's why I want you and Jonas to feed them every two hours. Make sure they drink plenty. I wanted to kick an outhouse down when I saw what they looked like."

Minnie agreed, "I wanted to helps you kick it down myself, honey child!"

Gabriel asked, "How about their skin?"

"I puts ointment on all de rashes and bits. Them boys had lots of varmints in de clothes and hair."

Gabriel suggested, "They have a long road ahead of them to recover. They must eat plenty, so they can heal and put meat on their bones."

Minnie said, "They'll eat, or I wills stuff it down their throats! When I told Mr. Gus what his family did for me, he cried."

Gabriel mentioned, "Fate or destiny can create many strange things."

Minnie smiled and commented, "What is meant to be wills happen, honey child."

"Amen, Ms. Minnie!"

"Yous a fine man, honey child!"

Gabriel added, "I'm going to sleep some. If anything happens get the doctor on duty. Tomorrow, we move westward. We'll pack up and give them an easy ride as best we can."

"Goodnight, sir."

The following morning, Dr. Hayden made his rounds. He changed Aaron's bandage and said, "The wound looks good. I'm sorry I had to amputate."

Aaron answered, "You did your best. Thank you for your kindness. I'm so tired, sir. When is this war going to end?"

"I pray very soon. I'm tired of treating wounds caused by war. Please eat and drink as much as you can, because you need it to heal."

"I will, sir."

Gabriel changed David's bandages and commented, "Your wounds look good, and so far, there's no sign of infection."

David asked, "Will I be able to walk?"

"Of course! You'll limp for a while, but it'll get better. Make sure to eat and drink plenty to help you heal."

"I will, sir. When Elisha comes back on duty, I want to shake his hand, because I'm glad my uncle's family was able to save them from the snowstorm. I've learned a lot these last few days, sir."

Gabriel suggested, "You will need to heal, and our nation will need to heal, as well."

David asked, "How is Micah and Gus?"

"They are resting and comfortable. I'm determined to save their feet."

David responded, "I don't know how Micah carried me with his feet in that bad of condition."

"I'd say pure devotion, love, and willpower kept him going."

Gabriel went over to Micah and Gus and said, "I've got

288

to change your bandages and look at my handiwork. I'll be as gentle as I can, but it's going to be painful, so I'll give you something for pain."

Micah stated, "We didn't want to give up!"

"You didn't; you simply found help for each other. There comes a time when fate takes over whether we like it or not."

Gus remarked, "I guess you're right. What's going to happen to us?"

Gabriel explained, "I'm going to get you well, first. Remember, you're my patients, not my prisoners. I've set up a hospital at Fort Monroe to care for the seriously wounded and sick soldiers from both sides. I'm planning on taking you with me to Fort Monroe where you can get the special care you need. When all of you have recovered, I'll escort you home."

Micah asked, "Why are you escorting us home, sir?"

"I want to meet your families and see what they need to get back on their feet."

Gus asked, "Can we write to our folks, because we haven't heard any word from them since the Wilderness?"

"Of course, I'll have Elisha get all of you some paper, pen, and ink to write your letters. I promise you they will be delivered."

"Thank you, sir!"

All the friends were able to finish their letters before the regiment moved out. That night they bivouacked near Buckingham Road. The following day, the regiment moved closer to Appomattox. The Union cavalry was able to capture food and supplies waiting for the Confederate army at Appomattox Station. Now, Gen Lee's army was boxed in, their escape route was blocked, and his men were starving. He couldn't make it to Lynchburg.

On April 9th, Gen Lee surrendered his tattered, exhausted army under generous terms. Gen Grant had 25,000 rations and feed for Confederate animals sent to Lee's army. The formal surrender would take place on April 12th where the Confederates would stack their weapons and flags.

When news reached the 53rd Pennsylvania of the surrender, Gabriel was changing Micah's bandages. The Union soldiers threw their caps in the air, danced, fell on the ground laughing, and hugged each other.

For the four friends, defeat and surrender were very difficult to accept. Tears ran down their cheeks, because they couldn't believe the war was over. They had sacrificed and suffered so much during those four years. What would become of them and Virginia?

The day after the formal surrender, Dr. Hayden's

wagon train of wounded and sick soldiers headed eastward to meet a train that would transport his patients back to Richmond. Their next stop would be City Point on the James River to be loaded onto boats that would carry them to Fort Monroe to get the extended care they needed.

On April 14th, Dr. Hayden's patients were loaded on the train headed for Richmond. Dr. Hayden's brother, Capt Oliver Hayden, had gathered 300 of the worst cases from the Confederate Libby Prison to be taken to Fort Monroe.

When the friends saw the devastation in Richmond, tears streaked their faces. There were long lines of starving, gaunt people waiting for food to be passed around. Piles of rubble marked where a once proud building stood.

On April 15th, the ex-prisoners of war from Libby Prison were transported to City Point and loaded onboard all sorts of boats to make their last journey.

Afterwards, the ex-Confederate patients were transported by boats to Fort Monroe. They arrived on April 17th where the Union patients were unloaded first. Once the task was completed, the ex-Confederates were unloaded, gotten settled into beds, and given a good meal.

Dr. Hayden came in later to change the friend's bandages. They noticed a change in the doctor's demeanor and wondered what it could mean.

Gabriel looked at the four and said, "President Lincoln was assassinated at Ford's Theater in Washington on April 14th. There's a huge manhunt ongoing to capture the killer, John Wilkes Booth."

President Lincoln's assassination

Instantly, the friends were terrified and on the verge of panic. Would they be murdered in their beds?

Gabriel suggested, "Don't be afraid! You're my patients, and I'll keep you safe! I have guards posted in this section, so nobody gets any twisted ideas. My colored orderlies and nurses are shaken, but this event will not affect the care for you. Elisha, Minnie, Jonas, Thomas, and Willis will be taking care of you. Any question?"

David pleaded, "We didn't have anything to do with this killer!"

"I know, David. It just proves the madness isn't over. President Lincoln didn't want to punish the South any longer, but I'm afraid the radicals in Congress will change that."

Lincoln's funeral train

John Wilkes Booth

Booth's route to the Garrett Farm in Caroline County,
Virginia

CHAPTER 19

Lt Parker rushed into his colonel's headquarters wondering if he'd done something stupid which meant a royal butt chewing. He snapped off a salute and stood at attention waiting for the ton of rocks to fall on his head.

"At ease, Parker!"

"Yes, sir!"

"Have you ever heard of a Dr. Gabriel Hayden?"

"No, sir!"

"Well, he must be a powerful son-of-a-gun. He has special orders signed by President, Secretary of State Seward, and Secretary of War Stanton. Whatever, he wants and needs, he gets!"

"Sir, could he be connected to Samuel and Silas Hayden?"

"Do you mean the railroad and shipbuilding tycoons?"

"Yes, sir!"

"I bet he is, because that would explain all this confounded commotion. I'm assigning you and your company this mission, because you know the Murphy families. There are five wagons outside loaded with food, supplies, and three cows. All of that is to be given to the Murphy's along with all these letters. Evidently, Dr. Hayden is treating their sons at Fort Monroe."

"That's incredible, sir!"

"If the Murphy families need any help doing some things around their farm, your company is to help them. Plan to stay for several days to help, if need be. Get your company busy packing up and move out as soon as possible."

"Yes, sir!"

"You've never let me down Parker, so don't start now!"

"I won't, sir!"

Lt Parker's wagon train was on its way within two hours. It was strange, but the men were looking forward to seeing the families, again.

Lt Parker smiled and thought, "I wonder how Hush Up Harry is?"

Leann was headed for the house with some eggs when she saw Yankee cavalry headed towards the house, so she raced inside and spread the alarm. The adults grabbed their weapons certain the cavalry was going to search everything looking for President Lincoln's killer.

Ty shouted, "It's Lt Parker and his company!"

Arthur and Homer went out on the porch wondering what the bejesus was going on. Lt Parker and his company dismounted, and Harry jumped off the porch, running towards Lt Parker. He picked up Harry and spun him around.

"How are you fine folks, today?"

Homer responded, "We're alright. We ain't hiding no killer!"

Lt Parker laughed and replied, "I know that, sir. We're on a very special mission. Do any of you know a Dr. Gabriel Hayden?"

Ellen fired back, "We ain't hiding him, neither!"

The company couldn't help but laugh, because Ms. Ellen was still her feisty ole self.

"I want you ladies to sit down, because I'm not good at picking up fainting females."

Ellen blabbed, "I don't faint!"

Homer added, "That's a fact, Lieutenant."

"Alright, but don't say I didn't warn you. I have here something you have been waiting for a very long time."

Ellen blabbed, "A notice saying the Yankees are leaving would make me very happy."

"It's better than that."

Ellen blabbed, "Just spit it out, you ornery cuss!"

Parker took out a packet of letters and waved it around.

He asked, "Does anyone know what this packet is?"

Ellen was just about ready to beat him over the head with a frying pan. She would have to go to church and ask forgiveness for what she was going to do to this infuriating Yankee.

Homer suggested, "Lieutenant, you better come to the point of this visit before my wife turns you into a biscuit."

"I have letters! Ms. Kathleen, this letter is from David Murphy."

She shot out of her chair, screamed, and grabbed the letter. The scene was repeated over and over, again, as they read their letters. Even Harry, Ty, and Teddy had letters to read. The tears started flowing from everybody. The troopers watched the scene unfold and couldn't help but swallow knots in their throats.

This scene of great joy, also, had a tragic side, because the folks learned that Clay had died of pneumonia in January. Homer held Ellen close as she mourned the death of her son.

When Ellen regained some of her composure, she asked, "Who is Dr. Gabriel Hayden?"

"He operated on your son, nephews, and Micah, and

he's taking care of them. Here's a letter from him, and he sent these wagons to you. They are full of food, supplies, feed for your animals, and three cows. We're here to help you do anything you need us to do."

Arthur commented, "We don't know what to say, because all of this is unbelievable. Why would this doctor do all this for us?"

Lt Parker answered, "Because he's an honorable, compassionate man, in my opinion. Don't forget, Judge Murphy, we're on the same side, now."

Ellen blabbed, "You're still a Yankee!"

"And you, Ms. Ellen, are still a true, southern lady who knows how to use a shotgun!"

She replied, "Darn straight I am, so don't git me riled up!"

Lt Parker handed out candy to everybody, gave the ladies brand new hair pins, and handed a box full of paper, pens, and ink to Homer.

"Write as many letters as you want, and we'll make sure your sons and husbands get them."

The sergeant asked, "Mr. Murphy, where can we set up camp after we help you put away all these things in the wagons?"

Homer pointed to an area, and then, the men got busy unloading the wagons. The families acted like it was Christmas, because there was flour, cornmeal, salt, sugar, coffee, bacon, hams, spices, potatoes, rice, molasses, and tea in the food department.

The ladies were sent all sorts of material and candles.

The feed was put away for the horses, cows, and chickens. Much to the men's surprise, there was even cut lumber in one of the wagons. Homer knew that would be enough to repair his fences. He was able to get two of the fallen trees off his pasture fence, but the third one was just too big to saw up and move. Maybe, he'd ask the soldiers for help.

The company put up their tents, unhitched the wagons, and got busy preparing beef for supper.

After everybody enjoyed a wonderful meal, Ty got out his banjo to play some tunes, so everybody could sing and dance.

They all had a wonderful time square dancing and singing. They laughed over crazy stories from their past as if they had been friends for years.

Parker commented, "Ms. Leann, you're a good dancer, and if you don't mind my saying, you have a pretty smile."

Leann blushed and said, "You're a good dancer and have a gentle smile. Do you mind if I ask you some questions?"

"Ask whatever you want to know, Ms. Leann."

"Are you married?"

"No, ma'am."

"Where are you from?"

"Frederick, Maryland."

"How old are you?"

"I'm 25 years old," he answered.

"What did you do before the war?"

"I worked for my brother in his saw mill. You see, my father died and left the family business to my brother. My father willed me a good sized inheritance. Suddenly, the war started, I joined the cavalry, and ended up here."

"Why did you join the cavalry?"

"Because I love horses! I want you to know there are many things the Union army did that I'm not proud of.

We have our share of blood-thirsty soldiers."

"The Confederate army has their share, too."

"Why would you say that?"

"Because we had a run in with Rebel deserters I consider scum."

"Some deserters leave to go home, because they're needed or just can't take the fighting anymore. Others are a mean bunch of outlaws, in my opinion."

"Amen to that," Leann added.

"When our regiment is mustered out, I'll go home for a while, so I can spend time with my mother. I see an opportunity in this area for my talents. I want to talk to your father and uncle about my idea to see what they think."

"I'm sure my father will listen to you, but don't be up to any Yankee tricks! My father can smell a bad apple into the next county!"

"I promise you no bad apples."

Homer and Arthur came over to Lt Parker to talk some turkey.

"I'm going to take you up on your offer to help," Homer said.

"What can we help you do, sir?"

"There's a huge tree blown down on part of my pasture fence line. We haven't been able to move it."

"Come tomorrow, we'll help you move it and cut some firewood."

Arthur chimed in, "It looks like we have a bargain!"

The following morning after a hearty breakfast, the men and soldiers tackled the huge tree down in the west pasture. With some hard work and ingenuity, the tree was moved, the fence repaired, and the tree chopped into firewood. The group agreed they could chop up a lot of the fallen trees in the woods for firewood. Another job for another day.

Before everybody enjoyed supper, Lt Parker talked with Homer and Arthur about his idea.

Lt Parker commented, "Your state has been ravaged by armies marching and fighting back and forth over the land. When I look at Stafford County, it looks like a wasteland, because all of the trees have been cut down. People who were farmers that fled this area to get away from the war will come back to overgrown fields, if they come back at all. Those fields will need to be cleared before a crop can be planted. So many have no house to come home to."

Homer responded, "I'm afraid many people won't come back. We have a friend who is a blacksmith and wheelwright. He left Fredericksburg, because he couldn't find enough work to make a living."

Arthur went on, "I left Fredericksburg, because I needed to keep my family safe from bullets, exploding shells, looters, and the enemy army. Right now, I don't have a job other than being a farmer."

Parker continued, "People need jobs to come back to. A lot of Virginia has no economy, no supply and demand, no law and order, no legal system, and worthless money."

Arthur added, "My sons are bricklayers and carpenters. I fear they won't be able to find work. How are they going to take care of their families?"

Parker responded, "I wish I had the answers. An economy takes time to develop; it doesn't start up overnight."

Homer suggested, "If you build a saw mill, your

business depends on people buying the lumber. How can they buy it if they have no money?"

Parker answered, "I've got to figure out how to make this work and be fair to all sides."

Arthur mentioned, "It could take decades to recover from this war. Virginia was ripped apart for four years, but it will take decades to repair and fix the damage. Don't expect people to be flocking to your business."

Parker suggested, "Sell or rent me eight acres. I have the capital to build a saw mill, office, and a home for myself. Sell me trees off your land I can turn into lumber and firewood. You set the price, and we'll work together on the selling price. Judge, your sons have the skills I need to build the mill and my home. I'll pay them a fair wage."

Arthur reminded, "Remember, Aaron has lost an arm."

"He can be my office manager and help me gather clients. I know several people around where I'm from that could be potential clients."

Homer suggested, "You might have to use the barter system for a while."

"I'm very open to that idea. I want to help the people here that have suffered so much."

Homer commented, "Micah Johnson was learning to be a bricklayer before the war. He could work with David."

Parker said with excitement, "See Mr. Homer, we're already creating jobs."

Arthur added, "Alright Lt Parker, I'll draw up a contract that will be fair to both of you. Are you willing to consent to pre-war prices, because things aren't worth a silver dollar, right now?"

"I agree. I'll telegraph you when I'm ready to settle here and get things built."

Homer suggested, "Make sure you contact us either way, because you might change your mind when you get back to Maryland."

"I will. One other thing, sir, can I call on Ms. Leann when I come back?"

Homer laughed and replied, "Lieutenant, that's up to her, but I want you to know she can be an excited hurricane, at times."

"Sir, that doesn't matter, because she has a gentle, loving spirit."

"Don't make her mad, because she'll kick you in your privates," Arthur added.

Parker laughed and responded, "I'll accept the challenge, sir."

Faces of the Civil War

CHAPTER 20

Dr. Hayden came in the door to check on his four patients. With him, he carried a big bundle of letters for all of them. He wanted to watch how they reacted to this special occasion.

He said, "Good morning, Thomas tells me your exercising and eating is going well. You are going to need lots of energy for this bundle I have."

Gus responded, "We're getting stronger every day, sir."

Gabriel started handing out the letters and watched Christmas unfold in the room. As their eyes raced across every page, they laughed, cried, and shouted for joy. Gabriel gathered from the conversations Hush Up Harry must be one special boy. He couldn't help but laugh about the kittens in the barn and the exploding outhouse.

Aaron shouted, "I'm a father!"

Gus looked at him like he had grown two more heads and fired back, "You can't be a father, Aaron. Is Deidre running around on you?"

Aaron told them the story about little Belle, and they were all shocked.

Gabriel remarked, "That's incredible! Your wife must be a very special woman, and I hope you'll love that little girl like she was your own."

Aaron replied, "You can bet on it!"

Micah shouted, "Congratulations, Poppa Aaron!"

David added, "She is a special gift given to you, Poppa Aaron!"

Gus blabbed, "I can't believe Leann kicked that

deserter in the privates. I didn't know Teddy was that good with a bow and arrow. Doc, can you believe my mother shot one deserter plum through the back door?"

"That was good thinking from everybody involved, because war can get downright evil. Your family did what they had to do in order to survive. You should be mighty proud of them," Gabriel said.

"We are, sir."

David asked, "When can we go home, sir?"

"How does the day after tomorrow sound?"

They all cheered and shed more tears of joy.

He went on, "Aaron, your arm has healed, so we don't have to worry about infection. David, your wounds have healed, and you're walking to build up your strength. The limp will get better as you get stronger. Gus, your feet have healed, and we don't need to worry about infection. You and Micah are walking slowly with some discomfort in shoes. You can continue to heal at home."

Micah said in a tearful voice, "My parents are dead from sickness. I don't want to go to Lancaster, because I have no future there. Grace still loves me, so that's my future. Somehow, I'm going to rebuild my home in Fredericksburg, so Grace and I can get married."

Dr. Hayden remarked, "Alright men, Elisha and I will escort you home. My uncle is providing a boat to take us to Fredericksburg where we'll pick up a cavalry escort to your folks. Elisha is bringing clothes and shoes for each of you."

David reminded, "Doc, we don't have money to pay for clothes and shoes."

Dr. Hayden replied, "You don't need to worry about that. You've eaten enough to put some pounds back on you, but you still need to gain more weight."

David mentioned, "I know our family will love to see Elisha, again."

Gabriel continued, "Elisha is excited about it. We'll stay a few days, and then, Elisha and I will need to get back to Fort Monroe, because I have two other patients that I need to escort to North Carolina."

Lt Parker and his company got lots of things accomplished during their stay with the Murphy family. He was anxious to get home and get things moving for his return to Virginia. He realized he was a very small fish in the ocean of devastation, but just maybe, he could help some of the people get back on their feet.

The sergeant poked his head in the tent and said, "Lieutenant, the colonel wants to see you in his office, right away."

Parker rushed over not knowing what to expect this time. He went into the colonel's office, snapped off a salute, and stood at attention.

"At ease, Parker. It looks like the cavalry gods have one more assignment before we muster out. Your company gets to escort Dr. Gabriel Hayden and four of his patients to the Murphy farm. I did some checking on the good doctor, and you were right. His daddy is Samuel Hayden, the railroad tycoon."

"I can't believe this! Gabriel Hayden could be living a lavish life style, but instead, he's operating on wounded soldiers and treating the sick."

"Parker, I was thinking the same thing, so maybe, Col Hayden is one of the honest people in this world."

"When do we leave, sir?"

"Dr. Hayden and his cargo arrive tomorrow, and

you'll be taking another wagon train of supplies with you. Get your men packed up and ready to go. Take plenty of supplies with you, because I don't know exactly how long the doctor will be staying."

"Does the Murphy family know they are coming?"

"No, but that's what the sons want."

"Sir, that's going to be one big surprise!"

"You know, Parker, you and I have been involved in some strange missions during this crazy war, but I think this one is the strangest. Not long ago we were enemies, and now, I wish them Godspeed and pray our nation can heal."

"I feel the same way, Colonel."

"Alright Parker, get busy, because I want you to meet them at the dock. Don't forget three of them will probably need stretchers."

"I'll take care of it, sir."

The four friends enjoyed their trip up the Chesapeake Bay. It felt so good to be away from trenches, hospital tents, and hospital beds. Their eyes soaked up the scenery, the wind felt good on their faces, and the water glittered like diamonds. Were they dreaming or was this really happening?

The closer they got to Fredericksburg the more anxious they became. Was this nightmare almost over?

Finally, the boat edged towards the dock, and the friends caught sight of an apparent Union cavalry escort.

When the boat was secured, Lt Parker went onboard, saluted Dr. Hayden, and said, "Dr. Hayden, my company is here to escort you and your patients to the Murphy farm. If there's anything you want or need, just let me know."

Gabriel replied, "It's good to meet you, Lieutenant. Right now, all of us could use a meal while our supplies are being unloaded."

"My colonel has arranged a good meal for all of you. Do any of your patients require a stretcher?"

"Yes, three will need them, because they're not as strong as they thought."

"Dr. Hayden, I have met the Murphy family before."

Gabriel asked, "Were you the Yankee who shot the bear?"

"Yes, sir!"

Gabriel laughed and said, "Come with me, so you can meet the men in private."

They walked into a room, and the four friends saluted the lieutenant and colonel."

Gabriel announced, "Fellows, this is the officer who helped shoot the bear, Lt Parker."

The friends broke out laughing as Parker went around shaking each man's hand. The ice was broken, and now, everybody could relax and be at ease.

Parker could see a strong family resemblance between David, Aaron, and Judge Murphy. Gus favored his mother a great deal. Micah was a good looking man, but Dr. Hayden had him beaten. Parker's sister would pass out if she saw him in person. He was one handsome and distinguished looking man.

Everyone enjoyed a good meal and talked among each other like they were old friends. What a difference a few weeks can make. Now, they were on the same side and very war weary.

CHAPTER 21

The following morning Lt Parker's wagon train started its journey. The friends didn't want a courier sent ahead to tell their families they were coming home. They wanted to see the looks on their families' faces when they saw them.

The night before Gabriel and Parker talked about his plans when he returned as a civilian. Gabriel realized his father and uncle ordered a lot of lumber from Parker's business. The colonel insisted on investing money in Parker's dream to make sure the business stayed operational for years to come. Also, Parker had his first client, because Gabriel would need lumber to build his clinic in Harrisburg, Pennsylvania.

The men were in the fields and everyone else was tending to their chores. Ellen was sweeping off the front porch when she caught sight of Yankee cavalry. She was just about ready to get her shotgun when she recognized Lt Parker.

She thought, "What is that pain in the behind up to, now?"

Parker rode up to her and asked, "How are you doing, Ms. Ellen?"

She fired back, "I was fine until I saw you. Now, you have ruined my whole day."

Parker laughed and asked, "Have you shot any bears, lately?"

She shot back, "No, but I'm fixing to shoot a Yankee lieutenant stone dead!"

He howled and commented, "Make sure you bury me

up there by the apple tree. That way I can talk to Hush Up Harry."

She fussed, "I will not, because you'd kill my apple tree. I'll throw your worthless hide in the river!"

"Aren't you afraid I'd kill the fish?"

"Lord deliver me! Talking to you is like talking to a snake! State your business and get on out of here!"

"I'm bringing your family one more wagon train of supplies before my regiment musters out."

She responded, "I'm grateful, Lieutenant. You didn't have to do this, because we're getting by."

He asked, "Can I bring up the wagons?"

"You're going to anyway, so get on with it."

The friends were hiding in one of the wagons with Dr. Hayden and Elisha waiting for just the right moment, because they wanted this moment to last for a lifetime.

When the wagons stopped near the house, the troopers gathered around Ms. Ellen to pay their respects.

She blabbed, "I see there are more cows, so I guess you plan to eat, and spend the night here?"

The sergeant remarked, "Would that be alright, ma'am? We sure did like your biscuits and cornbread."

"Alright, but don't wear out your welcome!"

"We won't, ma'am."

Gabriel whispered, "Your Aunt Ellen is giving the troopers fits."

David whispered, "She's all fuss and feathers like a peacock."

Gus whispered, "Mama will have the lieutenant fire off a shot to bring the men in from the fields. After that, let's slip out the back of the wagon real quiet like."

Gabriel whispered, "I love lots of intrigue and fuss!"

Ellen blabbed, "Snake fire off your revolver, so the men will come to the house."

The men heard the shot, grabbed their guns, and high tailed it to the house, because something must be wrong. Poor Leann about killed herself when she heard the shot. She dropped the bag of chicken feed in the barn, grabbed a pitchfork, and came running to do battle. When she got close enough, she realized it was Lt Parker.

She thought, "Why am I happy to see him? Darn, I want to hug him. Get control of yourself, girl!"

Parker commented, "Good day, Ms. Leann! Could you put the pitchfork down before you hurt somebody, honey."

Leann blushed ten shades of red and dropped the pitchfork. A trooper gave Lt Parker the signal.

He announced, "I've brought you a surprise, so look over there."

The four friends slowly walked out from behind the wagon.

Ellen's hands flew to her face, she screamed, and she raced towards Gus with open arms. She jumped into his open arms with tears running down her face.

"Sweet Jesus, thank you for bringing my boy home!"

"Oh Mama, I've dreamed about this moment, forever. I love you! This nightmare is finally over!"

Leann launched herself at Gus, and all three wept in each other's arms.

Kathleen picked up Andy and headed for the front door wondering what in tarnation was going on outside. She saw David and her heart started pounding. Tears flowed down her face as she ran towards her husband. David limped towards them and thought how beautiful his wife was. Andy had grown so much since he last saw him. They ran into each other's arms, kissed each other over and over, and wept tears of joy.

Grace dropped the bucket of water, because the shot scared the bejesus out of her. She came around the house wondering what all the commotion was about. When she saw Micah, she screamed and raced into his arms. They held each other close, kissed, and cried buckets of tears.

She begged, "Please, don't ever leave me, again!"

"I won't ever, again! You are my life. You kept me going when I wanted to give up, and your face kept me from going crazy."

Deidre finished changing Belle's diaper, picked her up, and headed for the front door wondering what on earth was wrong. She saw Aaron, broke into tears, and rushed across the yard towards him. They grabbed each other and smothered one another with kisses.

He said, "Oh, how I've longed for this moment. I don't want to ever forget it. Let me look at my daughter."

He beamed with joy and mentioned, "She's so precious. She's got the cutest little nose, and long eye lashes. You did the right thing, Deidre. She's ours, now."

Gabriel stood by Lt Parker and Elisha watching the scene unfold.

Gabriel commented, "You see, fellows, that's why I'm a doctor, so I can help people return to their loved ones."

Elisha added, "That's why I'm working for you, Dr. Hayden."

Parker reminded, "The men folk haven't gotten here yet. Colonel, don't you think Leann is a pretty young woman?"

"Of course, but is she like her mother?"

"No, she's more like her father," Parker mentioned.

"Are you sure, because she had that pitchfork ready to stick somebody?"

Parker laughed and said, "The pitchfork has a history."

"That's right! I remember, now. That came into play with the Rebel deserters," Gabriel added.

Parker looked at Gabriel and said, "Homer told me that Ms. Ellen likes to play mental chess with people, so she can get the upper hand."

Gabriel had a sheepish grin on his face, "I love matching wits with men or women. My meeting with Ms. Ellen should be quite interesting."

Elisha laughed and said, "I's going to enjoy watching yous sweet talk her, Doc."

Parker warned, "Here come the men!"

The men caught sight of the house and saw the Yankee cavalry and wagons. They had their weapons ready for a show down.

Harry shouted, "That's Lt Parker, Poppa!"

"Well I'll be, it sure is," Homer answered.

Now, the way the wagons were arranged the boys were hidden from plain view. The boys talked the women folk into hiding, so they could surprise their fathers and brothers.

Harry ran like the wind and jumped into Lt Parker's

arms. He hugged and tickled the boy until Harry giggled.

"How are you doing, boy?"

Suddenly, Harry noticed Elisha and another man he didn't know.

Harry yelled, "Elisha, you came back to see us!"

"It be just for a short visit."

Harry asked, "Who are you?"

"I'm a friend of Lt Parker and Elisha. You must be Hush Up Harry!"

Harry asked, "How do you know my nickname?"

"They told me all about you!"

Harry asked, "Are you an important officer?"

"Not really, young man."

Harry mentioned, "If Lt Parker likes you, then you're welcome around here."

"What would you do if Lt Parker didn't like me?"

Harry answered, "I'd throw you off our land with a pitchfork!"

"Ouch! I promise I'll be good!"

Harry ordered, "You better be, because I'm real good at surprise attacks!"

Ty, Teddy, Homer, and Arthur greeted Lt Parker, Elisha, and Gabriel with hugs, handshakes, and back slaps. The troopers gathered around the men to make the surprise complete.

Parker said, "We brought one last wagon train full of supplies before we muster out."

Homer remarked, "Lt Parker, that wasn't necessary."

He teased, "But it was, because we brought you another surprise."

The boys stepped out from behind the wagons

holding on to the women folk.

Arthur shouted, "Sweet Jesus, it's my sons!"

Teddy and Arthur ran to David and Aaron even though their eyes were full of tears and their chins quivered. They had prayed so hard for this day to come. Could this horrible ordeal really be over?

Between tears and sobs Arthur said, "I'm so proud of you, Grace, and Teddy. A man couldn't ask for better children. Thank God you are safe."

David commented, "Aaron and I are proud of all of you. We know what you did to help keep our families safe from those deserters."

Teddy sobbed and answered, "I wanted to make you proud of me!"

Harry, Ty and Homer rushed to Gus. They, too, had tears running down their cheeks.

Homer shouted, "Thank God, you came home, son! We thought this day would never come!"

Ty pleaded, "Don't ever go away, again!"

Harry cried, "You can't leave anymore, Gus! You can't fight no more wars!"

Gus hugged his brothers and promised, "I won't."

Harry chimed in, "I got a woman picked out for you, Gus. If you don't marry her, I will."

Gus asked, "And who might that be?"

Harry blabbed, "Eva Moss."

Gus asked, "Are you serious? She's a skinny, homely looking girl."

Harry fired back, "She ain't no more!"

Gus turned to Ty and asked, "Is Harry serious?"

Ty replied, "She's a real looker, now. In fact, I might marry her!"

"Well, right now, I have more important things to do."

The troopers couldn't help but shed a few tears

themselves. Each one prayed their homecoming would be this sweet when they were mustered out and returned home.

Ms. Ellen walked up to Lt Parker and scolded, "You knew our loved ones were in the wagons. Why didn't you tell us?"

"Now, Ms. Ellen, surprises are so much better!"

"I ought to take a frying pan to your behind. I almost had a heart attack."

Ellen hugged Elisha and said, "I thought you and your family were headed north."

"We crossed the river, and all of us found work with the Union army."

Homer asked, "What kind of work?"

"Jonas and me is orderlies in the hospital. Minnie cooks and takes care of de wounded and sick soldiers."

Homer commented, "That's wonderful, Elisha. Did you take care of Gus and the others?"

"I's sure did! De men worked really hard to gits on their feet!"

Ellen chimed in, "I'm so grateful you took excellent care of our boys."

"I's wanted to pay yous back for all your kindness!"

Homer added, "You certainly did that and more."

Ellen looked at Gabriel and asked, "And who might you be, Colonel?"

Gabriel smiled, took Ellen's hand, and kissed it while Ellen turned twenty shades of red.

She thought, "My, my, you are one handsome scoundrel!"

"I'm Dr. Gabriel Hayden. I came along for the ride."

Suddenly, Ellen remembered the letter he sent her, she rushed into his arms, burst into tears, and kept thanking him for saving the boys.

Gabriel had a hard time dealing with crying females, because he didn't have a clue about what to say or do. Therefore, he patted her shoulder and told her the boys were recovering well.

Arthur commented, "Dr. Hayden, we are so thankful you took care of our boys. My family will always pray for your safety. The war is over, and all of us want to heal."

In a flash, Gabriel was surrounded by four more crying females. He looked at Lt Parker for help, but the lieutenant just grinned like a fat cat eating fish.

Homer remarked, "We'll never be able to repay you for all the supplies you've sent to us. If there's anything we can do for you, just tell us and we'll get it done."

Gabriel answered, "All I ask is you help the men recover and get back to work. The lieutenant told me about his plans for a saw mill, and I'm his first customer."

Parker jumped in, "He needs lumber to build his clinic in Harrisburg when he's mustered out."

Gus responded, "We'll make sure you get the lumber, sir?"

"That's good to hear. Aaron, let me see your daughter."

Gabriel took little Belle into his arms and said, "She is a special little girl given to you for a reason. She's kind of like a gift to start a new life together."

Deidre replied, "We're starting a happy new life together."

Gabriel kissed Belle's forehead and gave her back to

Deidre. Then, he walked over to David and picked up David's son, Andy.

He remarked, "You are a handsome young man. I pray you will love your Poppa and help him heal."

Andy jabbered, "Poppa, home from de war."

Elisha brought a box over to Gabriel and pulled out a wooden horse.

Gabriel handed it to Andy and said, "One of my patients carved this while recovering from wounds. I think this is just perfect for you."

Andy grabbed the horse laughing and ran to his Poppa.

David said, "Thank you, Doc. We will always cherish it."

Gabriel addressed the group, "When I was told the story behind finding your loved ones, my faith in goodness and devotion was restored. Micah and Gus walked on cut, blistered, and mangled feet carrying David and Aaron who were unable to walk. Soldiers from my regiment found them exhausted and collapsed on the road. Micah and Gus couldn't walk anymore, but they continued to try to drag their friends. When my men found the four, Micah begged them to help his friends and not shoot them. In my opinion, this is the finest example of devotion and love. That's why I had to bring them home to you in person."

David spoke up and said, "The four of us would like you to know we'd serve alongside of you anywhere."

"Thank you, David. That means a lot to me. Gus there are some things in this box you want to hand out.

Gus picked up Clay's knife and said, "Ty, I want you to have Clay's knife, because I know you'll always cherish it."

Ty took it, put it to his chest, and wiped tears.

Gus picked up Clay's cap and a button from his uniform and said, "Harry, I want you to have these to cherish."

Harry took them, ran into his father's arms, and cried.

Gus picked up Clay's Bible and gave it to his mother and gave his father Clay's pocket watch.

Lt Parker said, "My men will unload the wagons, set up camp, and get busy on beef for supper."

Gabriel added, "Our patients need to rest."

So, the families went inside along with Elisha and Gabriel. The ladies passed out apple cider and made some biscuits and honey to snack on before supper. The friends knew they were back home when they bit into those hot, honey biscuits fit for a king. Gabriel and Elisha enjoyed their fair share of them, too.

Believe it or not, it wasn't long before the four men were fast asleep in their loved ones arms. Gabriel answered a lot of questions about their wounds and how to care for them.

Once all the supplies were put away, the ladies started their part of supper to go along with the beef.

After eating supper, Ty got out his banjo, so everybody could enjoy singing and dancing. Gabriel had a fine time and noticed a lot of sparks between Lt Parker and Leann. Could there be a budding romance starting up?

Ellen asked, "Are you married, Dr. Hayden?"

"No, ma'am. The war put a stop to romance."

She remarked, "I can't believe you don't have a train

load of women after you, because you're one handsome man. If I was twenty-five years younger, I'd be after you."

Gabriel laughed and added, "The women after me are rich, conceited, husband hunters. All they're after is money. I want a woman who loves me, not my money."

"Well, I pray you find her. Mark my words, you need a wife with some fuss and feathers to match that rascal attitude of yours."

"I was thinking the same thing."

Ellen teased, "I hope you have a passel of children just like my Harry!"

"Ah Ms. Ellen, do you mean like Hush Up Harry?"

They both giggled like children getting into mischief.

Ms. Ellen continued, "There are so many tragic stories in these parts. Dr. Lawson lost two sons killed in action, Delilia Musselman lost two of her three sons, Leannh White sent six sons to war and only two returned, and Wren Saunders's wife died in July 1864 leaving seven children behind. Thank heavens, the cavalry discharged him to come home."

"Stories like that have affected families all over the North and South. It breaks my heart that a whole generation has been sacrificed by this war. Both sides have so many battered souls who need help to heal. I'm hoping my clinic can save some of them."

"I'm sure it will. Bless you for taking in Elisha's family. They are good people, and they will work hard for you."

"Elisha's family will be an important part of my clinic."

"That's good to hear."

"Lt Parker is letting Arthur know their homes are

vacant, now. He made sure the homes weren't badly damaged. There are a few repairs needed, but otherwise they're ready. I took the liberty of ordering supplies for the three homes, so they can move in."

"That's wonderful, but they are welcome to stay as long as it takes."

"You did a fine thing, Ms. Ellen. Not everybody would take in that many folks."

"For Pete's sake, you rascal! They are my family! We look out for each other."

"You sure did that!"

Ellen asked, "What are your plans for tomorrow?"

"The troopers want to cut lots of firewood for you and do some fishing. They tell me you serve the best fried fish in Virginia!"

"A fish fry sounds good."

"The following day we must leave, because I need to get back to Fort Monroe."

"I want you to know, you'll always have a special place in my heart," grinned Ellen.

"Even though I'm a rascal!"

"It's a special place for rascals!"

The two had another private giggling session between a rascal and a fuss and feathers queen.

Two days later, the cavalry wagon train left the Murphy farm fighting back tears. None of them had been hugged and kissed this much in their entire lives. They left behind a wagon and team accidently on purpose, because the family could sure use it.

A few days later, Abner Moss's family stopped by for a visit. George helped his daughter get down from the wagon.

Gus asked Ty, "Who is that woman?"

"It's Eva!"

Gus fired back, "That can't be Eva! This woman is stunning!"

Harry blabbed, "We told you Eva was all growed up!"

The Moss family walked towards them, and Gus's mouth dropped open.

Gus thought, "She can't be Eva!"

George and Luella greeted Gus with open arms.

Gus asked, "Who is this lovely lady, George?"

He answered, "It's Eva! Don't you recognize her, Gus?"

Harry slapped his arm and said, "Gus don't think Eva is Eva!"

George and Luella laughed until their sides hurt.

Eva held out her hand and said, "I'm so glad you are well and finally home. We've missed all of you."

Gus stood there transfixed, so Harry slapped him, again, and lifted Eva's hand to his mouth. Ty slapped him from the other side getting mighty irritated. Suddenly, Gus snapped out of it and kissed her hand.

He said, "Sorry Eva, but you took my breath away. You are gorgeous!"

"Thank you Gus! That was mighty kind of you to say."

Ellen invited everybody to come inside, so they could visit with the whole family.

Gus just stood there, so Harry and Ty slapped him, again.

He snapped out of it and said, "Eva take my arm, and I'll escort you inside."

As they left, Harry looked at Ty and blabbed, "Sometimes, Gus is real stupid!"

Ty fired back, "Amen to that!"

Faces of the Civil War

Coming Soon

Enemies on the Battlefield

Randolph Waverly was one of the aristocratic planters that owned a several hundred acre plantation in Alabama next to the Chattahoochee River.

As the storm clouds gathered over the nation concerning the conflict over free states and slave states, Randolph finds out that two of his six children question the status quo of a planter's way of life.

When these two children become a problem to deal with, he sends them to live with his sister in Louisville, Kentucky.

When the South secedes from the Union, Randolph's sons and nephews split and become enemies. Over the next four brutal years of total warfare, the 5th Kentucky Infantry Regiment and the 33rd Alabama Infantry Regiment will cross paths several times on the battlefield.

How many will survive? Does an act of compassion help heal the wounds of war? Will Randolph ever take his two banished children in his arms, again?

ABOUT THE AUTHOR

Faye M. Benjamin was born and raised in Virginia where she still lives with her husband and black cat "Spooky."

Faye graduated from Woodbridge Senior High School in Woodbridge, Virginia and went on to study secondary education at James Madison University majoring in history. After graduating from college, she taught history in the Prince William County School System.

She enjoys creating her stories and wants to share that joy with those people who love to read.

Readers can visit her website at www.fayebenjamin.com for the latest information on her current and future releases.

So, readers sit back, relax, laugh, and enter her Freestone's world of murder, mystery, intrigue, humor, and the paranormal.

For those readers who enjoy Civil War novels, she is writing a series of human interest stories about the Civil War that are part fact and part fiction.